GHOSTS
of CORNWALL

Peter Underwood
President of the Ghost Club

Bossiney Books

First published in 1983
by Bossiney Books
St Teath, Bodmin, Cornwall
Designed, typeset and printed in Great Britain by
Penwell Ltd, Parkwood, Callington
Cornwall

ISBN 0 906456 73 8

FOR

Air Commodore R. Carter Jonas
of Fowey
in friendship

PLATE ACKNOWLEDGEMENTS

Front cover by Ray Bishop
Drawings by Paul Honeywill
Pages 7, 9, 13, 20, 29, 55, 58 Ray Bishop
Pages 25, 42, 72, 73, 76, 95 Alice Lennox-Boyd
Pages 51, 63, 74, 81, David Wood
Pages 45, 52, 66, Woolf-Greenham Collection
Pages 43, 67 Richard Isbell
Page 33 Murray King
Pages 5, 37, 96, back cover The Author
Page 8 Royal Institution of Cornwall

About the Author

Peter Underwood has been President of the Ghost Club (founded 1862) since 1960 and has probably heard more first-hand ghost stories than any man alive. A long-standing member of The Society for Psychical Research, Vice-President of the Unitarian Society for Psychical Studies, a member of The Folklore Society, The Dracula Society and a former member of the Research Committee of the Psychic Research Organization, he has lectured, written and broadcast extensively. He took part in the first official investigation into a haunting; has sat with physical and mental mediums and conducted investigations at seances, been present at exorcisms, experiments at dowsing, precognition, clairvoyance, hypnotism, regression; conducted world-wide tests in telepathy and extra-sensory perception, and has personally investigated scores of haunted houses.

He possesses comprehensive files of alleged hauntings in every county of the British Isles and many foreign countries, and his knowledge and experience has resulted in his being consulted on psychic and occult matters by the BBC and ITV.

Born at Letchworth Garden City in Hertfordshire, he now lives in a small village in Hampshire. He is Hon. Librarian of The Savage Club, 9 Fitzmaurice Place, Berkeley Square, London, W1 where he can be contacted.

In 1982, Peter Underwood made his debut for Bossiney with *Ghosts of Devon*. An immediate bestseller for the cottage publishers, it was featured on BBC television from Plymouth, and discussed on DevonAir.

Here Peter Underwood completes a haunting and haunted double with *Ghosts of Cornwall*. 'While compiling this book, I have met some fascinating people and heard some remarkable stories,' he writes. 'While, for the sake of completeness, I have included, briefly, some of the better-known ghost stories, I hope I have something fresh to say or something to add to each of these accounts. In the main, however, I have tried to find new and little-known stories of ghostly encounters . . .'

Herein lies the strength and the appeal of this journey across mysterious Cornwall.

By the same author

A Gazetteer of British Ghosts (Souvenir Press and Pan)
A Gazetteer of Scottish and Irish Ghosts (Souvenir Press and Fontana)
Ghosts of Devon (Bossiney Books)
Ghosts of Hampshire and the Isle of Wight (St Michael's Abbey Press)
Ghosts of North West England (Collins/Fontana)
Haunted London (Harrap and Fontana)
A Host of Hauntings (Leslie Frewin)
Into The Occult (Harrap and Tandem)
Deeper Into The Occult (Harrap)
Hauntings—New Light on Ten Famous Cases (Dent)
The Vampire's Bedside Companion (Leslie Frewin and Coronet)
The Ghosts of Borley (with Dr Paul Tabori) (David and Charles)
Ghosts of Wales (Christopher Davies and Corgi)
Lives to Remember—A Casebook on Reincarnation (with Leonard Wilder) (Robert Hale)
Dictionary of the Supernatural (Harrap and Fontana)
The Complete Book of Dowsing and Divining (Hutchinson)
A Ghost Hunter's Handbook (Hutchinson/Sparrow)

BIOGRAPHY
Horror Man—The Life of Boris Karloff (Leslie Frewin)
Life's a Drag—A Life of Danny La Rue (Leslie Frewin and Star)

AS EDITOR
Thirteen Famous Ghost Stories (Dent's Everyman's Library)

IN PREPARATION
Ghosts of the National Trust (Macmillan/National Trust)

The Author ▶

Introduction

Cornwall is a land of mystery where, even today, in some hamlets and away from the busy roads, there is an atmosphere not altogether of this world. Once over the strangely winding Tamar and into Cornwall the visitor enters a mystic land and it is indisputable that visits to this Celtic County leave an indelible impression on the mind. Those who are lucky enough to return again and again never really escape from the enchantment of the place—or want to.

Cornwall is full of ghosts. There are strange stories of diminutive figures, of silent and brooding forms, of invisible influences, of repeated appearances, of haunted houses and ghostly cities; it is a rich hunting ground for the ghost seeker and for those who appreciate the odd, the miraculous and the inexplicable. The ghosts of Cornwall are a varied bunch indeed and if the recounting of their stories gives as much pleasure to the reader as the research gave to the author he will be more than satisfied. While compiling this book, I have met some fascinating people and heard some remarkable stories. For the sake of completeness, I have included, briefly, most of the better-known ghost stories, but I hope I have something fresh to say or something to add to each of these accounts. In the main, however, I have tried to find new and little-known stories of ghostly encounters and this compilation should make a worthy companion volume to my recently published *Ghosts of Devon*.

And, needless to say, I am still looking for genuine ghost stories, everywhere, but especially in beautiful Cornwall.

The Savage Club   Peter Underwood
Fitzmaurice Place
Berkeley Square
London W.1.

GHOSTS of CORNWALL

Bedruthan

You catch your breath when you see Bedruthan Steps for the first time, and thousands of people every year visit the sixty acres of spectacular clifftop scenery overlooking the beach and countless miles of ocean. But few realise that this was once the site of tin and iron mines and a very ancient castle. Here the slurred and weary

At Bedruthan Steps (right) the 'click-click' of miners' picks has long been heard.

tread of long-dead miners in their heavy boots and the 'click-click' of their picks has long been reported by quiet visitors who have no knowledge of the area.

In 1981 I met a local man who had heard the clicking sound many times, sounds that he and others accept as paranormal, although the sceptical say that the sounds are caused by underground water. No such explanation is possible, however, for the grey forms that have been seen here at night, disappearing where no human form could go.

Bodmin

Lanhydrock House, near Bodmin, has the gentle ghost of a little old lady. Dressed in grey or possibly black, she haunts the Gallery and the Drawing Room, the oldest parts of this lovely house and the area which escaped the disastrous fire of 1881.

The Grey Lady, as she is known, has been seen walking down the Gallery, the great room of the house running the length of the north wing. She is also often seen sitting on one of the gilded beechwood armchairs in the Drawing Room and is at first taken to be a real person; but as soon as she is approached, the figure disappears. Nobody knows the identity of the ghost although it has been suggested that she is Isabella, the second wife of John, 2nd Baron Robartes (1608-1685). The Robartes family owned Lanhydrock from 1620 until the property passed to the National Trust in 1953.

The 'female presence' that has been distinctly felt on occasions in Her Ladyship's Room would appear to be a different visitor from the past; possibly the Lady Robartes who, at the age of sixty-eight, was rescued by means of a ladder from an upstairs window at the time the house was virtually gutted by fire, and who died a few days later, never having recovered from the shock. Her husband could not get over the tragic loss of his wife and his home and he died the following year.

During one of my visits to Lanhydrock, in 1981, Tim Belton, at that time Assistant Administrator, told me that on several occa-

The grey lady haunts the gallery of Lanhydrock. ▶

sions the odour of fresh cigar smoke had been noticed appropriately enough in the vicinity of the Smoking Room on the ground floor; a smell that is quite unmistakable and completely inexplicable. Possibly some psychic echo from the past.

Bolventor

Isolated and romantic, high up on Bodmin Moor, stands Jamaica Inn, immortalised by Dame Daphne du Maurier when she used it as the setting for her well-known novel of smuggling days, which was later filmed under the same name. Unexplained footsteps, believed to be those of a young man who was murdered at the inn, are said to echo round the stone floors at regular times of the year, and mysterious hoofbeats have been reported on certain nights. During the month of August, a few years ago, the midnight hoofbeats were said to be heard repeatedly. Sometimes too, especially on foggy nights, the figure of a man on horseback has been seen waiting outside the inn. Jamaica Inn, on the old coach road which runs from Launceston to Bodmin, was once the haunt of smugglers and highwaymen, and, although the road, changed and improved over the years, now bears the title of A30, the inn itself has not changed greatly in the last hundred years.

My wife and I look in at Jamaica Inn from time to time, park our car in the cobbled courtyard, over which stagecoaches used to rattle, the inn sign swinging and creaking above in the breeze. We make our way through the great wooden door beneath the porch leading into the lounge, that large stone-flagged room containing a wonderful collection of swords, muskets, lanterns and old brass hanging from the ceiling. In one corner a doorway leads into Mary's Bar, so-called after Mary Yellan, the heroine of Daphne du Maurier's story. It is at this bar, many years ago, that a stranger stood drinking a pot of ale that he was fated never to finish, for, upon being called outside, he put his half-empty tankard on the bar and disappeared into the night.

In the morning his murdered body was found out on the moor, but the identity of his assailant has never been discovered. More than one landlord has heard ghostly footsteps tramping along the passage to the bar—are they those of the murdered man returning to

Bodmin Moor: 'Isolated and romantic . . .'

finish his drink?

Some years ago there was a great deal of correspondence in *Country Life* about a strange man who was often seen by many people sitting on the wall outside the inn; he never spoke or moved and his description seemed, from everyone's account, to have been so similar to that of the murdered stanger that it was thought that he must be the dead man's ghost.

Jamaica Inn certainly has an atmosphere. It is reputed to be over five hundred years old and still contains some of the original walls of local granite, in places six feet thick: is it possible for past events to impregnate these old stones that must have seen smugglers and wreckers in past days? Even today there is a brooding atmosphere here.

A few years ago a couple reported seeing a ghost in their bedroom when they spent one night at the inn. Shortly after falling asleep they awoke to see a man standing by the bedroom door, the last room on the right in the upstairs corridor. He seemed to be wearing a three-cornered hat and a long, old-fashioned, tight-waisted overcoat. As they watched he slowly moved past the end of the bed and disappeared through a large wardrobe. Both witnesses said the room was icy cold while the figure was visible. Next morning, when they related their experience to the landlord, he did not seem in the least surprised and merely said: 'The old boy always goes through the wardrobe when he returns to that room.'

Bossiney

A first-hand account of a haunted farmhouse in Bossiney is to be found in *The Folklore of Cornwall.* Here I paraphrase the salient points.

The informant was about eleven years of age when she and her sister stayed with their parents at the house, said to be one of the oldest buildings in the area. One morning the two girls awoke to find that some large and heavy framed paintings had been removed from the wall in the night and now stood with their backs to the room, on the floor. The informant's mother and another guest examined the pictures at the time and agreed that neither of the children could have been responsible; the paintings were simply too heavy.

A few nights later the informant's father, who was sleeping in an adjoining room, was awakened by the rattle of a pitcher and bowl which stood on the deep window ledge in the room occupied by the children. On entering the room he found the informant sitting cross-legged on the ledge, apparently staring out to sea. When he asked her what she was doing she said she had seen a little, bent old man, who had whispered to her and she could not remember anything else.

Next day the owner of the house was asked whether she had been disturbed by the noise during the night. She wanted to know exactly what had happened and afterwards said she hadn't said

St Nectan's Glen is haunted by a hooded figure dressed in grey. ▶

14

anything earlier in case they wouldn't stay in the room, but that part of the house was supposed to be haunted by the ghost of a hunchback who had lived there and he was in the habit of sitting at the window in question, cross-legged and staring out to sea.

The family stayed at the farmhouse for three years running. On one occasion the mother and one of the daughters had gone into Launceston with some friends, leaving the informant, who suffered with car-sickness, with her father. The weather was dull and miserable and in the afternoon, feeling thoroughly fed-up, the girl went upstairs to her bedroom and there saw an old man sitting hunched-up in a cross-legged position on the window ledge. For the rest of their visit she had terrifying dreams and a very real fear of the haunted bedroom. She was totally unaware of the fact that it was supposed to be haunted until some years later.

Nearby St Nectan's Glen has a strange and indescribable air of unreality; it has been called 'one of the most beautiful corners of North Cornwall' by Michael Williams who has chronicled the experiences of several local people: a writer, who lived nearby and claimed that he often heard the sound of chanting monks at night; a local man who said he had heard the sounds of sobbing and weird laughter; and Kathleen Everard who talked of beautiful organ music emanating from an empty building . . .

Saint Nectan who, after being decapitated, is credited with picking up his head, is reported to have appeared at Hartland Church in Devon and there are stories of the Saint warning sailors of submerged rocks by ringing a silver bell from his tower. From the lane by the Rocky Valley Hotel, you follow the indicated path, treading the route that pilgrims trod in the sixth century when they went to pray at the shrine of St Nectan. Today the hermitage and the whole glen that bears the Saint's name are haunted places.

When I was there in September, 1982, both my wife and I found the atmosphere overwhelmingly expectant and it was easy to accept the stories of strange figures appearing and vanishing inexplicably; of cats and dogs being worried and acting strangely for no apparent reason; of snatches of music, footsteps, whispering and chanting. In particular I was told about a hooded figure dressed in grey, with a blue lining to the hood, very kindly-looking but somehow troubled, and I like to think that on occasions this troubled Saint returns to the place he loved—perhaps to ascertain the whereabouts of the

16

treasure that was reputedly buried with him and his sacramental vessels somewhere in the bed of the river at this idyllic spot.

Botatan near Launceston

A curious story is told by the Reverend John Rudall; a story, seemingly of a spirit earthbound by an unconfessed sin.

A young woman named Dorothy Dinglet (or Dingle) died here and although little is known of her life and loves, a family named Bligh could be best described as acquaintances of the dead woman, no more.

There were two sons in the Bligh household, one a young man, the other a schoolboy. Almost immediately after Dorothy Dinglet's death the elder son left the area and is heard of no more; it is not known whether there is any connection between the two events although there are suggestions that Dorothy died in childbirth, the father being the elder of the Bligh brothers.

About three years later the younger boy, who crossed a certain field on his way to school each day, was troubled by a ghostly form which he met each morning.

The form was that of a young woman who walked towards him, pointing to something in the distance. He recognized her as Dorothy Dinglet but she took no notice of him, just steadily gliding over the grass and passing out of his vision on the opposite side of the field.

The constant sighting of the visionary figure began to unnerve the boy and his father approached the Reverend John Rudall, then curate at Launceston. The priest heard the boy's story and readily agreed to accompany him next morning on his way through the field. Much to his astonishment he too clearly saw the figure and he prepared himself to speak to it but was overcome with fear until the figure had passed.

Rudall then obtained permission from his Bishop to exorcise the ghost and leave being at length granted he went alone to the field, prepared to wrestle with the earthbound spirit he was convinced he was dealing with.

His preparations indicated a somewhat curious and certainly deep knowledge of matters not usually known to country clergymen for he wore a ring engraved with the *Scutum Davidis*; he carried a

17

crutch of rowan; he traced a circle on the grass and drew a pentacle within the circle, setting his rowan stick at the point where the five angles intersected; and, facing north, he waited for the ghost to appear.

When the phantom form duly put in an appearance John Rudall read aloud from a parchment commands which he repeated three times and then he addressed the ghost in Syriac, a language, he says, 'which is used where such ones dwell and converse in thoughts that glide.'

He then induced the ghost to enter the circle and gently asked her why she was not at rest. She replied that it was because she had committed a certain sin in life; she confessed the sin and the priest 'released her troubled spirit'. The following morning, according to John Rudall, he met her again and after certain commands she disappeared towards the west and was not seen again; but evidence in my possession suggests that the ghost of Dorothy Dinglet was seen subsequently on a number of occasions and there are those who believe that her unquiet spirit still walks on misty mornings.

The exorcism of the ghost of Dorothy Dinglet is supposed to have taken place in a field called Higher Brown Quartils and for years there was a path running through the field that was known as 'Dorothy Dinglet's Path.'

Callington

Nearby Cotehele House belonged to the Edgcumbe family from 1353 until it was acquired by the National Trust in 1947, but in 1553 the family moved to Mount Edgcumbe, eleven miles away, and from then onwards the house was only occupied occasionally; thus it escaped major alteration, enlargement or rebuilding and the parts open to visitors are much as they were more than three hundred years ago. The furnishings of the house have also remained largely undisturbed, providing perhaps an ideal setting and environment for ghostly perambulations.

Exorcism at Botatan: 'Rudall prepared to wrestle with the earthbound spirit . . ' ▶

Yet beautiful Cotehele is usually free of ghostly manifestations apart from the occasional powerful whiff of perfume that has repeatedly been reported by visitors and many members of the staff, in the east wing and elsewhere. The administrator and others at the house tell me that the odour is suggestive of a herbal fragrance and is, so far, quite inexplicable. At least one visitor, totally unaware that such a fragrance had been repeatedly experienced before, reported an overwhelming odour of herbal fragrance accompanied by 'plaintive music' in the oldest part of the house.

Of course there are legends associated with Cotehele. One story goes that in some long-forgotten quarrel in the dim and distant past

Cotehele: '. . . an odour of herbal fragrance accompanied by plaintive music was reported.'

a man was killed beneath the archway leading to the present entrance at Cotehele and the spot where he fell and expired remained forever marked by an irremovable bloodstain . . . small wonder then that there are vague stories too of a ghostly form being seen hereabouts seemingly, from the costume, dating back to the seventeenth century.

The 'bloodstained' stone was moved to the little bridge by ancient Cotehele Quay and painted over, obscuring a curiosity and perhaps placating a ghostly manifestation. The presence of red ironstone in the area must suggest that the so-called 'bloodstained' stone was in all probability a particularly vivid natural display of the veins in the stone which can look very much like blood when it is wet.

Mrs Phyllis Julyan has resided for many years at Cotehele and she tells me that for her the house has always had a lovely atmosphere and while she is not able to feel or see ghosts and is quite convinced that the people who once lived there were happy and contented individuals, nevertheless she was good enough to relate two ghostly episodes.

The first occurred during the last illness of the 5th Earl of Mount Edgcumbe when a nurse from Tavistock was sitting by his bedside. She noticed a woman dressed in white pass through the room and since, at that time, anyone could walk right round the house through the various rooms surrounding the courtyard, she took no notice, thinking it must be the housekeeper. Later she encountered the housekeeper and noticing that she was dressed in black, the nurse said to her: 'Have you changed your dress because when you passed through the Earl's room surely you were wearing a white dress?' The housekeeper told her that she had certainly not changed her dress and furthermore she had not been near the Earl's room that morning and she added: 'You must have seen the ghost . . .'

Another more personal experience befell Mrs Julyan at Christmas, 1980, when a friend telephoned her after calling to wish her the compliments of the season. On the telephone this friend asked Mrs Julyan whether a young girl was staying with her, a girl with long hair and wearing a white, flowing dress; for she had encountered such a figure going down the private staircase as she had left Mrs Julyan. No such person was in fact staying at the house and no one of that description was ever traced.

In such a lovely old house as Cotehele it must seem likely that ghostly emanations from the past still linger and are occasionally visible or sensed in some way by people who are perceptive to such things.

Camborne

After one of my broadcasts about ghosts and haunted houses, Mrs M.A. King of Camborne wrote telling me about a curious experience that she had on Easter Monday, 1971, and I do not think I can do better than quote from that original letter and the subsequent correspondence:

'I take the dog for walks along the country roads not far from here and on this occasion, as we were climbing a long and steep hill, I noticed a woman some twenty yards or so further up the hill, about to mount a bicycle. As we were both on the same side of the road (a busy one, I might add), it was obvious that she would be passing quite close to me in a minute or so. Unfortunately, in the split second that I looked down at the dog and then raised my eyes again, she had completely vanished—bicycle and all.

'The road was especially steep at the place where she had been and it was very wide too. If she had changed her mind and gone back the way she had come, she would have had to cross the road, turn the bicycle round and begin pushing it up the hill. The only alternative to this would have been for her to cross a rather wide grass verge and go through into a field; but there was no gate at that particular spot and the hedges were very high. In either of these events I would have been bound to see her.

'I often try to recall what she looked like and as far as I can remember she was about thirty-five or forty years old, slight with a sallow complexion, poorly dressed in a grey cardigan and I think she was wearing a hat.

'. . . As near as I can remember the time would be between half-past three and four o'clock. The place was a continuation of Tehidy Road, which runs alongside the Red River and joins the main road somewhere close to Tehidy Hospital.'

The phantom knight appeared to be cut off at the knees . . . ▶

As Mrs King says in a subsequent letter it would be interesting to know whether a person answering such a description has been killed on the road at that point and perhaps even more interesting if it was found that other people had seen a female cyclist who disappeared near Camborne.

Camelford

The ghost of part of a knight has been seen at a Queen Anne house overlooking the square. One night a previous occupant had found herself suddenly wide awake in the middle of the night and she saw the clear figure of a knight standing by her bed; he appeared to be quite solid and normal in every way except that the figure ended at the knees, which appeared to rest on the floor. Subsequent enquiries established that the house, which has traces of Tudor cellars and walls, has been altered many times over the years. The floor level in the room where the ghost was seen had, in fact, been raised, suggesting that the phantom knight was appearing exactly where it had always appeared. One wonders whether anyone who happened to be in the room below would have seen a pair of metal-clad legs sticking out of the ceiling! I understand that the figure was readily visible by virtue of the fact that a bright moon shone into the room through the window.

Nearby Slaughter Bridge, traditionally the scene of King Arthur's last battle, has a strange atmosphere to this day. Upstream from the bridge, on a bank close to the water, an oblong slab of moss-covered granite is regarded by some as King Arthur's Gravestone.

Whether in 537 the Battle of Camlam took place here, in which Arthur and Mordred fell, experts disagree but some bloody battle must have taken place here to be perpetuated in the name of the bridge. Perhaps it has something to do with the misty and unexplained figures that have been seen occasionally crossing the bridge and disappearing into the history-laden air that surrounds this strange place.

Incidentally, after his death King Arthur's spirit is said to have entered a chough (the red-legged Cornish crow) at Slaughter Bridge and bad luck was said to come to anyone who killed this bird which is now extinct.

Finnygook Inn—
renamed in honour
of their ghost.

Crafthole

The beach at Whitsand Bay was the scene of many a smuggled cargo and the well-known free-trader who had headed a gang of like-minded men was named Finny. Their headquarters was a public house on the Torpoint to Looe road, then known as the New Inn.

One night Finny's luck ran out. He and his followers were surprised by revenue men and in the resulting short but sharp skirmish Finny was killed.

Thereafter his ghost was reported to frequently revisit the sene of his earthly triumphs and final desperate struggle and in 1950 the brewers, I am told, renamed the inn in honour of their ghost. Today the old New Inn has become The Finnygook.

Forrabury

Ghostly bells with ghostly chimes have long been associated with the waters here. It seems that new bells for the local church were conveyed by a blasphemous sea captain who, on arrival, forgot the sacred nature of his cargo to the extent that he cursed the elements for his tempestuous journey—whereupon a violent storm broke and mountainous waves rolled over the vessel and it sank with all hands in sight of the village inhabitants.

As it foundered the bells in the ship's hold rang for the first and last time for the people of Forrabury; except that whenever a storm is brewing in the area a peal of phantom bells reportedly echoes from beneath the waves and to this day no bells hang in the belfry of the local church. I have talked with people who have not only heard the ghost bells but have also allegedly seen phantom boats with phantom crews rowing silently to the spot where the ship sank.

Gulval

Following a broadcast entitled 'Strange to Relate' concerning a phantom motor vehicle, Mrs Marion Grace Paul wrote to me from St Ives and subsequently was good enough to supply me with full details relating to a haunted house at Gulval.

In the late 1950s Mrs Paul and her husband were house-hunting and they became interested in a large corner house that was for sale. One sunny afternoon they set out to see over the house. While waiting for someone to show them over the property Mrs Paul went down a few steps on the ground floor and was looking out of a window, one hand on the windowsill, when she suddenly had an overwhelming feeling that the place had a very evil atmosphere and she knew immediately that it would not be a good place to live. Furthermore this unexpected impression of the house was accompanied by an intense shock or charge that seemed to travel up her arm from the hand on the windowsill: a powerful shock that left her arm feeling paralysed. They soon left the house and went to Penzance to call on Mrs Paul's parents to see whether they could find out anything about the history of the house. Mrs Coulson Paul, a Penzance person by birth, said immediately in reply to their enquiry: 'Oh, didn't you know a woman was murdered there?'

Shortly afterwards Mr and Mrs Paul, still intrigued by the atmosphere inside the house at Gulval, related their experience to a long-standing friend who lived at Mousehole. He remembered that a friend of his, who had been looking for accommodation, had obtained a room there at the top of the house. One evening, Mrs Paul's friend told them, he had gone to visit his friend and as he opened the downstairs front door a small black dog had slipped inside and run up the stairs ahead of him and disappeared into a room where the door stood open. Feeling responsible for letting the dog into the house, he thought he should find it and put it outside again but there was no sign of the dog in the empty room where he had seen it enter seconds earlier and there appeared to be no place whatever that it could be concealed.

He now became aware of a very curious atmosphere and when he eventually located his friend, who seemed obsessed with the house and would hear not a word against it, he nevertheless advised him to move as soon as possible for his own good.

Shortly afterwards this friend who resided in the haunted house was returning home one night when he apparently saw a car coming straight towards him; he swerved to avoid it and drove into the path of another car and was killed in the ensuing crash. His companion in the car described the 'phantom' vehicle to the police. Other witnesses said that the car swerved as if to avoid something that they could not see and so ran into the other car, with fatal results.

A resident of Marazion has revealed that efforts were made to exorcize the house at one time, following repeated appearances of a ghostly 'white lady' seen leaving, crossing the road and making her way to the beach where, it was said, she had committed suicide.

A man who now lives in Sussex visited the house to call on a friend and encountered a lady in old-fashioned riding habit, standing at the top of the stairs—a figure that vanished inexplicably. Another witness saw a small black dog which disappeared when she tried to touch it.

I may say that I have the names and addresses of all the people concerned in these experiences but out of respect for their privacy I am not revealing any further details but I am hoping to conduct an investigation at the house in the not too distant future.

Gwithian

Nearby Hell's Mouth, where there are cliffs two-hundred-and-seventy-five feet high, is reputed to be haunted by the sounds of a suicide's cries.

Many and varied are the tales told and written about The Mouth of Hell but the haunting appears to correspond with the story of a black-hearted rogue who threw himself headlong into the angry waters at the foot of the towering Black Cliffs.

It was wild country hereabouts in days gone by and not a few of the tunnels that run underground at the foot of the cliffs at Hell's Mouth were useful for hiding smuggled goods of one kind or another. A freetrader, whose descendants still live in Cornwall, resided in a nearby valley with his sister and he and a boon companion prospered from the proceeds of a nefarious life until his friend was suddenly arrested. He was hurriedly taken under escort to Launceston, where he would certainly have been hanged, but neither the prisoner nor the escort arrived at Launceston. News travelled fast among the freetraders and the two men thought it wise to set their backs on Cornwall for a while.

The freetrader's sister was as gentle as he was wild and he loved her more than life itself but she knew that he had to leave the country. Amid tears he set off, promising to return one day.

Some time later, raiders came ashore under cover of a threatening storm, pillaging the countryside, firing the villages and homesteads and taking away the cattle and the people they had not slaughtered.

When the freetrader returned he found only smouldering ruins where once his home had stood and the ravaged body of his murdered sister. Driven to distraction by the loss of the one person he loved so dearly, he hurried to the high cliffs to see whether there was any trace of the murdering raiders but they had all gone. As he stood with the roaring sea at his feet and the sound of seagulls in his ears, he became overwhelmed with despair and threw himself over what is now called Hell's Mouth. And ever since it is said that when the wind is in the north west and heavy seas are rolling in from the coast of Labrador, as they were that night long, long ago, then the cries of the broken-hearted freetrader echo again among these ageless rocks.

A few years ago some mining students camped upon the rocks below Hell's Mouth and afterwards they said they had heard fierce yells and snatches of old sea shanties echoing from the caves and tunnels beneath the Mouth of Hell.

Helston

Nearby Godolphin House, former home of the Earls of Godolphin, is reputedly haunted by Margaret Godolphin, according to an article in the *Western Morning News* and several other published sources.
The house was the home of the Godolphin family for centuries and the ghost of the unhappy Margaret, who died in childbirth in 1678, is alleged to have been sighted on numerous occasions, usually in the vicinity of the entrance hall of the house, where she has been seen to emerge from a tiny closet, long since sealed up, and move out onto the terrace and into the avenue of old trees and there 'to walk

Hell's Mouth: '. . . the cries of the free trader echo against the ageless rocks.'

disconsolately among the shadows'. The body of Margaret Godolphin is buried in the church at Breage.

The eminent historian, Dr A.L. Rowse, once spent a night at Godolphin sleeping in the guest room, perhaps within an arm's length of the sealed closet, and in an Elizabethan bed too. He had scarcely fallen asleep before he was awakened by 'the unmistakable swish of a woman's silk dress' sweeping through his bedroom!

There are said to be five escape routes in the house that dates back to Tudor times, designed for the safety of Charles II; today the names King's Room and the King's Garden remind us of turbulent days.

Antony Hippisley Coxe tells me that nearby Jew's Lane is haunted by the ghost of a Jew who hanged himself from a tree and was buried beneath the road but a ghost bull has long been associated with the area although why this should be so nobody seems to know.

The Beehive Inn, Coinage Hall Street, is thought to be haunted by the ghost of a young man who was murdered there over a hundred years ago. The fact that some witnesses have described the figure as being dressed in 'modern style' need not necessarily rule out the murder victim: some suits of a hundred-and-fifty years ago are strikingly similar to those worn by some young people today and in any case most witnesses of this apparition, which is usually seen an hour or so before midnight, say the form is 'rather shadowy'.

Ladock near Truro

In the valley of the Tresillian River nestles the haunted church of St Ladoca. Nearby, Tresillian Bridge was the scene of the final surrender of the Royalists to Parliamentary forces in 1646 and here the terms of peace were arranged.

The restored Early English church with its Norman font and monuments seems peaceful enough to the casual visitor but at certain times and especially, I am told, at mid-evening, various people on various occasions have thought that another person has entered the church with them, only to find themselves alone once they are inside. At other times, out of the corner of the eye, a shadowy figure has been seen inside the church; a figure or form that disappears whenever it is approached, dissolving swiftly into nothingness.

Mr A.M. Hammett, who has long lived in the vicinity, tells me that the regular bell-ringers have often thought that an additional ringer has joined them during their weekly evening practice but this has proved not to be so. 'Many times,' he tells me, 'a large number of people over the years have seen the unidentified ghost figure' and now it is more or less accepted that the ghost comes to listen to the bell-ringing. 'I myself did not think that such a thing could happen', Mr Hammett continued, 'but I have experienced it myself on a number of occasions.'

He says there is no feeling of coldness or atmospheric change when the ghost form is seen and he feels sure that it is a benign presence. A legend is beginning to grow in the neighbourhood that the ghost is that of a past churchwarden or bell-ringer who served there for many years and whose personality returns on still summer evenings to the church he loved when the bell-ringers are making their quiet way to the church they also love in their turn.

Lamorna

The old farmplace of Trewoofe, overlooking lovely Lamorna Valley, has many legends and several ghosts. The present owner, Mrs Margaret Powell, tells me she has never seen a ghost at Trewoofe although 'perceptive' friends feel them and, while the stories of ghosts and unusual happenings are, mostly, stories, nevertheless they are based on historical facts and a good knowledge of the locality. 'As a historian,' says Mrs Powell, 'I know the names of everyone who lived in my house back to 1270 and while I do not take such stories seriously, it is easy to see how these legends came to be passed on . . . Trewoofe was a medieval Manor House and had its mill—the leat still runs above the house and the site of the millpond can still be seen—not an unlikely place for two children to drown in the time of the Crusades.'

This is a reference to one of the most persistent ghost stories associated with Trewoofe; that the ghosts of two drowned children are seen gathering wild flowers by the banks of the former millpond.

One of the many legends tells of Squire Lovelis out hunting one evening when he spied a white hare and, calling his hounds, he gave chase. The hare fled into a large opening in the ground, a Cornish *fogou*, or inland cave. Lovelis followed and found the hare changed into a witch and part of a coven presided over by a demon. The squire recognized the demon as his wife's lover and roundly cursed him, whereupon the whole assembly turned on him and when he eventually emerged from the cave at midnight, followed by his hounds, baying wildly and foaming at the mouth, he was quite mad. The *fogou*, according to the 1975 publication, *The Folklore of Cornwall*, is still haunted by Lovelis's raving spirit and Mrs Powell tells me that there is a *fogou* in the woods below Trewoofe and that she has been told that it is situated on a ley-line.

Land's End

Marc Alexander has told me a strange story about a lonely cove here that is the haunt of a phantom dog whose bite can kill.

It seems that in the sixteenth century the Emperor of China sent, in the care of one of his daughters, a pair of Pekinese dogs; animals that had been bred as early as the eighth century especially for the Chinese Imperial family and owned by them exclusively.

A dog and a bitch made the journey, the bitch travelling in a large ivory chest, and during the voyage she gave birth to puppies: baby Lion Dogs of China. Off the Cornish coast a violent storm drove the English ship that carried the Princess and the dogs across the Channel, towards the cliffs of Land's End. The superstitious crew turned on the yellow-skinned girl and blamed her presence for the unexpected storm.

They broke into her cabin and threw the unfortunate girl and her dogs overboard but not before a sailor had been bitten by one of the terrified dogs.

The body of the Chinese Princess was washed ashore in a cove beside the ivory box but for some time the local people would not go near the strange yellow girl whom they thought must be a foreign demon. When they did eventually open the box all the dogs were dead except for one which soon expired. The girl and the dogs were buried in the cove. Meanwhile word came that the sailor who had been bitten by the dog aboard ship had died and word soon spread that the lonely grave should be avoided because it was guarded by the ghostly Pekinese dog.

From time to time a local man, braver than the rest, would approach the grave at dead of night and dig for the ivory chest which it was thought might contain treasure, but each time invisible teeth closed upon the hands or ankles and invariably the would-be grave-robber died. Eventually even the bravest treasure-seeker left the haunted cove to its ghost.

The last recorded incident dates from the middle of the last century when a boy was playing on the beach and came across a piece of carved ivory hidden in the sand. As he reached for it he felt something bite him although nothing was visible. On his arm were teeth marks and within a few days the boy was dead.

A few miles south at Hella Point there have been sightings of a pair of phantom lovers. Back in the days of sailing ships Nancy

Land's End: There is 'a lonely cove here that is the haunt of a phantom dog whose bite can kill.'

(some versions of the story have her named Polly) and a seaman named William were sweethearts but Nancy's father, a Porth-gwarra farmer, disapproved of the young man and so the couple would meet secretly at a spot that became known as Sweetheart's Cove.

William had promised that after one more voyage he would leave the sea and after he had gone Nancy watched and waited for his return from a spot on Hella Point that became known as Nancy's Garden. But the months went by and there was no news from William and no sign of the return of his ship.

One moonlit night Nancy stood for hours, looking out over the sea, and then she wandered down to the cove and sat on a rock. A neighbour saw the sad-faced girl sitting gazing at the sea and she saw too that the tide was fast coming in but the girl made no move to leave her lonely vigil. Fearing that Nancy might let herself drown in the melancholy of her loneliness, the woman began to climb down towards the cliff to see what she could do. When she arrived on the shore she was surprised to see another figure seated on the rock beside Nancy: had William's ship returned and was this the long-awaited lovers' reunion?

Quietly watching she saw the waves come higher and higher. She screamed and shouted to warn the pair but the lovers either did not hear or did not wish to heed her call. She saw the waters wash over them and they walked out to sea, their hands entwined and each looking into the other's eyes . . .

No trace of Nancy was ever found and soon word came that William's ship had foundered on its homeward journey and had sunk with all hands. And from time to time there are reports of a ghostly pair of lovers walking hand in hand along the shore at Porthgwarra Cove, figures that vanish inexplicably.

Launceston

After one of my broadcasts on the fascinating subject of 'Haunted Houses' I received a letter from Mrs Denise Buckridge of Dockacre

'The sad faced girl sat gazing at the sea.' ▶

House, Launceston, during the course of which she told me that the five-gabled Elizabethan house, built into the side of a hill and occupied by her family, had an interesting haunting associated with it.

Visiting beautiful Dockacre in the company of my much lamented friend, James Turner, I heard the odd story of the alleged haunting and the even odder story of the moving walking sticks.

We explored the fine staircase and heard the story of Nicholas Herle who is said to have shot his wife Elizabeth, accidentally or by design, on this very staircase. It is said that for more than two hundred years a large and irremovable bloodstain was to be seen on the second tread up from the hall. Some years ago the staircase treads were removed and all traces of the 'everlasting bloodstain' were lost although there are inhabitants of Launceston today who remember seeing it.

Nicholas Herle, a noted barrister of the day and twice Mayor of Launceston, in 1716 and again in 1721, died in 1728 at Hampstead. Pastel portraits of both Nicholas and his wife Elizabeth in the present dining-room have hung there since before Elizabeth died, in somewhat mysterious circumstances, in 1714. They comprise part of the property and estate and are sold with the house. Elizabeth's monument in the Church of St Mary Magdelene refers to her death 'by starvation or other unlawful means'. At one time there were secret passages leading from Dockacre House to either the Church or the nearby castle and one identified passage entrance is visible in the cellar.

It is said that Elizabeth went mad and her husband had her locked away in a small upstairs room and there proceeded to systematically starve her, one of the prescribed cures for madness at the time, but he seems to have overdone the treatment and when she was near to death the frenzied Elizabeth escaped from her room and was almost at the bottom of the stairs on her dash for freedom when her husband accidentally or intentionally shot her dead.

One might have expected her ghost to haunt the house but it is the ghost of Nicholas Herle that has been seen here, usually in the main hall, notwithstanding the fact that he died more than two hundred miles away; and he is also credited with playing a flute whenever a death is about to occur in the house. I examined the flute which cannot be played by mortal man since one end has long been blocked-up and it has been made into a walking stick.

The author examines the flute stick at Dockacre House.

Walking sticks seem to have a strong association with Dockacre House. There is a tradition that every owner of Dockacre hands on to his successor a walking stick to add to the collection housed there. I saw the collection which now numbers thirteen, including the 'flute stick'. The sticks are kept in a sack in the attic and, I was told, they are themselves subject to supernormal interference if they are not kept in a particular order, for with much rattling they will then sort themselves out into the correct sequence. They are an interesting collection and include a sword stick, a cane and a stick with a detachable knob capable of secreting poison.

The Reverend Sabine Baring-Gould lived here at one time and he wrote about the ghost in his book, *John Herring,* where he has the ghost appear to two of his characters at the front door.

When I was at Dockacre I learned that previous owners of the place have reported pictures falling from the walls without any apparent reason and of strange bangs and crashing noises at night; of tappings and the sound of unexplained footsteps and of the inexplicable opening and closing of doors; but today Dockacre is a happy house and untroubled by the flute-playing 'Man in Red' of former days. Yet still something of the old atmosphere remains for some visitors.

Mrs Buckridge tells me that there have been two rather strange occurrences while they have been there. A woman was visiting Launceston after an interval of fifty years and asked whether she could see the house again as a relative used to live there. She recounted that on occasions when she went to visit, as a child of about eight years old, she would get as far as the main staircase and suddenly and for no apparent reason feel ill and faint. After this had happened a couple of times she was taken away and never returned to the house. She knew nothing about the reputed ghost at the time or the allegedly violent death on the main staircase.

The other incident concerned a friend who had brought her sister to the house without telling her anything about the ghost or the legend of the sticks. When this girl, aged about twenty, went upstairs and saw the sticks, she turned very pale and became icy cold and rushed down the stairs and out of the house!

The churchyard at Launceston has long been said to be haunted by a *kergrim*—Cornish word for a ghoul; an unpleasant ghost associated with burial places, and I am told that the priory ruins harbour the ghost of an Augustinian, black-cowled monk, last seen in 1975. A similar figure was reportedly seen at the now demolished Walk House by Dr Arthur Budd when he lived there and by a later occupant, a boy who had no knowledge of the figure seen by Dr Budd.

Not far from Launceston, amid the rolling countryside, stands a centuries-old house, once a farmhouse and later a holiday home, but it stands on 'ill-wished' land and has long been regarded as an unlucky and haunted place.

Years ago it is said that a man hanged himself in the kitchen in the depth of some forgotten despair and not so long ago a military man reputedly died there in mysterious and unpleasant circumstances.

My informant, a local person of good standing who has known the house and the locality all her life, once had permission to use the telephone when the occupants were away. She accordingly went to the house one evening but just as she was about to use the telephone she heard heavy and regular footsteps sounding on the ceiling over her head, apparently emanating from the room above. She knew there was no human being up there and she hurriedly left the house and never did make that telephone call!

Some years later, one Christmas, she and her mother were invited to the house for Christmas dinner and at the height of the festivities her mother, sitting next to her at table, turned and said sharply, 'Don't shake my chair, dear'; a moment later my informant's own chair was violently shaken and, although they diligently sought for the cause or reason, they never found any explanation. These are just two of the many odd and never explained incidents that seemed always to be occurring.

Another occupant of the house, who also died there very suddenly and at a young age, had a dog which habitually slept over a barn, some twelve feet above ground level, reached by means of some stone steps. Occasionally the dog, a friendly and quiet animal, would visit my friendly informant who lived nearby. One night, around midnight, she and her mother heard something scratching at the door and when they went to see what it was, they found the dog from the big house—but he was shivering and cowering with fright. They let the animal inside and settled it down for the night but in the morning it simply would not go home. Time and time again it was taken up the drive but halfway along it would stop, dig in its feet and refuse to go any further. So the dog passed into the possession of my friend and it lived a happy life for another six years and is now buried in the garden but for the rest of its life it would never go all the way along the drive to the house where it had lived for years, nor would it go near the barn where it had slept all its life until that night when something frightened it almost out of its wits. That night it had gnawed its way out of the barn, jumped some fifteen feet to the ground and raced down the drive away from the 'something' that it never forgot.

That very odd house, with a very odd name, crouches expectantly in the lush countryside, seemingly waiting for something to happen . . .

Linkinhorne

Nearby Rillaton is credited with one of Britain's oldest ghosts: a phantom Druidic priest.

Legend has it that he would often be seen by travellers beside an ancient tumulus near Rillaton Manor, offering passers-by a drink from a golden cup—a magic cup that could never be emptied.

One night a weary traveller tried to drain the cup and when he found it was impossible to do so, he became annoyed and then angry throwing the wine into the face of the phantom, he remounted his horse and resumed his journey: soon afterwards he and his horse were found dead at the bottom of a ravine.

This seems all very legendary and unbelievable but oddly enough Rillaton Barrow was excavated at the beginning of the last century and the skeleton of a man was unearthed and, beside it, a golden cup. The cup is now preserved in the British Museum.

Looe

A ghostly white hare is reputed to run from Talland to Looe and there vanish at the door of The Jolly Sailor Inn.

The phantom animal is supposed to be connected with a young girl who committed suicide. In an effort to make up for her wickedness, she seeks to help the inhabitants of this ancient port, for the transmogrified form is said only to appear when misfortune is about to strike or some danger threatens the town. The original Ye Olde Jolly Sailor Inn was a white-washed waterside haunt of pirates and smugglers, but the story of the girl who killed herself, the reason she runs to the Jolly Sailor, and why she should appear as a white hare, nobody knows.

Looe Island

There is a story, going back to the 1850s, concerning a lady who, while staying for a holiday at a farm here, was frightened when she encountered the ghostly figure of a tall, aristocratic-looking man

◄ A phantom Druid standing by an ancient tumulus offered travellers a drink from a golden cup.

Above. Looe Island where a lady encountered a
ghostly figure in a bluish haze. A ghostly white
hare runs from Talland to Ye Jolly Sailor Inn at Looe (right).

with beautiful hands and long fingers, who appeared enveloped in a
kind of bluish haze, walked across the room and disappeared
through the opposite wall.

Later the woman heard that several people who had stayed at the
farm had reported seeing blue lights that no one could explain but
she never heard of anyone else who had seen the ghostly figure.

Some years afterwards a skeleton was unearthed on the island
and was discovered to be that of a tall man with exceptionally long
fingers.

Lostwithiel

Nearby Braddock Down saw Cromwell's army suffer a rare defeat
on 19 January 1643 and ever since, on the anniversary of that
battle, the thunder of horses' hooves have been reported to echo
mysteriously about the battle area: a curious cyclic phenomenon
that has parallels with Edgehill (23 October 1642) and other
battlefields. And, as at Edgehill, there are those who have caught a

Ye
Jolly Sailor
Inn
over 500 years old

glimpse of war-weary soldiers, Roundheads and Royalists, disappearing into the wintry gloom.

Ludgvan

Here a tall figure, swathed from head to foot in white, has frightened many people; a figure that always seems to disappear in the vicinity of a churchyard wall.

One witness, a stranger to the area knowing nothing of any reputed ghosts, became lost in the middle of a storm one night. As he told himself he would make enquiries at the next house, he became aware that he was being followed by a tall and white figure, a form that disconcertingly kept the same distance behind him, no matter whether he slowed down or increased the speed of his pace. At length the traveller found himself along a churchyard wall, over which he could see wet gravestones gleaming in the moonlight; he looked behind him and saw the figure that had been following him for perhaps ten minutes; suddenly it turned and disappeared in the direction of the graveyard. Another witness described seeing a hooded figure in the graveyard gateway. Similar stories created something approaching panic among the local people a few years ago and no one would go anywhere near the burial ground after dusk.

Some writers have connected this tall, white form with the publicly-hanged Sarah Polgrain (see entry for Mount's Bay) but there is really very little evidence to support such a suggestion, especially as reports of a tall, white shape that frequents the churchyard were in circulation before the Sarah Polgrain case.

Marazion

St Michael's Mount, that romantic fortified monastery, has several ancient legends associated with it and a bed that no child can sleep in.

The legend includes a one-eyed giant and, appropriately, a vision of St Michael himself, but for more recent psychic manifestations

44

Ludgvan: '. . . a tall figure swathed in white
seems to disappear in the vicinity of a churchyard wall.'

Lord St Levan tells me that he can only confirm that a four-poster
bedstead, dating from the seventeenth century, has a very curious
atmosphere and many people have remarked upon the fact. The
bedstead is decorated with figureheads of Spanish ships that were
wrecked off the Cornish coast hereabouts and no child, it seems, has
ever been able to spend a night in the bed.

A ghostly 'white lady' has long been said to haunt the vicinity of
Marazion Green where she would materialize to the consternation of
late travellers for sometimes she would accompany them for a while
before fading away and disappearing as mysteriously as she had
originally appeared. I have not been able to trace the possible
identity of the apparition.

Morwenstow

Psychic disturbances at nearby Tonacombe Manor have been described by Michael Williams who visited the fine fifteenth-century house with David Waddon-Martyn. Reported phenomena have included knockings upon several windows and doors, apparently from *within* the house; the sound of material being dragged across the floor; the misty image of an old lady in Stuart period costume; the form of a short, bald man, dressed in a black coat and breeches; and an Elizabethan woman carrying a big bunch of keys.

There are some grounds for thinking that the ghostly old lady may be Katherine Kempthorne who could have died at Tonacombe in 1613 and lies buried in Morwenstow Church.

Some years ago strange happenings at Stanbury Manor were reported to me by the then occupant, Mr T.A. Ley, which seemed to centre on a large cedar chest which was thought to be of Spanish origin and possibly came to this country with the Spanish Armada. Carved on the lid and four sides were representations of dismembered heads and headless bodies. The proprietor of the shop where it was purchased had said that there was 'something queer' about the chest: wherever it had been placed in the shop, things fell off the walls in the immediate vicinity. Mr Ley, until he could decide on a permanent place for the chest, had it put in the armoury.

The next morning, while he was walking through this room, six guns fell off the wall together—the wires were not broken and the hooks were still intact and secure.

The chest was moved into the Ley's bedroom and the same evening while Mr Ley was helping his wife to hang some curtains on a four-poster bedstead, a picture fell down and struck him, although he was fully eighteen inches from the wall at the time. Oddly, the heavy picture hit Mr Ley on the head so lightly that he hardly felt it and it left no mark.

Next day three more pictures fell off the walls of the room containing the chest while Mr and Mrs Ley were actually present. Two days later four more pictures came down in the drawing-room, where the chest had been moved, again while both the occupants of the thirteenth-century house were present; one of these pictures went backwards through some stout pipe panelling into a 'secret' passage. (Photograph: back cover).

Next day another picture fell in the drawing-room and in every case no hook or wire was broken although many of the pictures that fell for no apparent reason were damaged.

The local press dubbed it 'the case of the poltergeist chest' and a former curate of Newlyn West, recognizing the published photograph, related the following story concerning it.

Many years ago there resided in the village two ladies who owned the chest. They were both elderly and stone deaf and used to communicate by means of messages written on notepaper and passed to each other. They lived as recluses and were rarely seen in the village by the local people. During their lives they had collected a great deal of junk and thought that they possessed a valuable collection of antiques. They decided to put these objects up for sale and the curate went along to examine the articles. He found it very difficult to do business with the deaf ladies since they wrote their usual notes and expected him to reply in the same way. On making enquiries among the inhabitants the curate learned that the two sisters when young had gone on a visit to some friends and, arriving very late, they retired without unpacking their trunks which they placed on a chest that stood in the bedroom allocated to them. In the morning as they awakened, their attention was immediately drawn to the chest for, although weighed down by the heavy trunks, the lid was opening! They went over to the trunk and looked inside and what they saw was so horrible it is said that they were struck stone deaf on the spot. What they had in fact seen they would never reveal.

On hearing this story I immediately remembered the account of a haunted chest that was published in a volume of 'authentic narratives' in London in 1882 entitled *Ghostly Visitors*. This story concerned a hard-headed surgeon who went to visit a friend at his house in the Midlands. The bedroom allocated to him was spacious but dreary and in one corner stood a large carved chest. After examining the outside of the chest, moved by some unexplained impulse, the surgeon raised the lid. Inside he saw a man lying with his throat cut. With an exclamation of horror and surprise the surgeon let the lid fall but almost immediately raised it again. To his great astonishment the chest was empty! On mentioning his experience to his host the next morning, the latter stared at him in amazement and informed the surgeon that a former occupant of the room had committed suicide and had been found in the chest in the condition now described by the visitor.

If it *was* the same chest, was a sight such as the surgeon witnessed horrible enough to strike two young ladies deaf? We know that a woman's hair turned white at Ilford in 1943 following an accident, and Marie Antoinette is said to have suffered in the same way. One wonders whether on re-opening the chest the ladies, too, found it empty; a fact which might well account for their never revealing what they had seen.

As far as the Leys' chest is concerned, Mr Ley told me that there were no further disturbances and he wondered whether it all had anything to do with the death of a member of the Ley family that seemed to coincide with the total cessation of anything unusual happening in the vicinity of the carved Spanish chest.

Mount's Bay

Here, according to the reports of many fishermen, a ghost voice calls the words 'I will . . . I will' over and over again amid the occasional sound of church bells far out in the bay.

More than a hundred years ago there lived at nearby Ludgvan an old man named Polgrain and his young wife Sarah, who tiring of her elderly husband, became the lover of a young sailor known as Yorkshire Jack.

Sarah murdered her husband with arsenic and nearly got away with it. The local doctor was satisfied that death had been due to natural causes and signed the death certificate accordingly but after the funeral as Sarah and her young lover lived together openly, rumours of foul play began to circulate and eventually the body of old Polgrain was exhumed and was found to be full of arsenic.

Sarah was arrested, charged with murder, found guilty and sentenced to be hanged. On the day of the public execution Sarah, as a last request, asked that Yorkshire Jack might be allowed to accompany her to the scaffold. Together they mounted the gallows platform and just as the rope was being placed around Sarah's neck,

'Ever since that day on the gallows
Sarah had never left him alone.' ▶

the couple embraced and kissed for the last time and spectators, near the gallows, heard Sarah say, in slow and measured tones: 'You will—you promise you will?' to which Jack answered, nervously but firmly, 'I will—Sarah—I will . . .'

Soon after the execution of Sarah Polgrain her ghost was seen in Ludgvan; once in the churchyard where she and Jack had been in the habit of meeting and once or twice on the high road between Penzance and Hayle, where she and Jack had walked so many times and planned so many happy days ahead of them. But it was Jack who, apparently, saw the ghost of Sarah most often.

The once happy and carefree young sailor changed almost overnight and before long he was morose, short-tempered, restless and unhappy and he developed a habit of constantly looking over his shoulder. To one or two old friends he confided 'She gives me no peace . . . she is there, wherever I go . . .' And they knew he spoke of Sarah.

Even at sea Jack was haunted by his dead lover. His shipmates chaffed him for constantly turning and rebuking something they could not see but at night as he lay in his hammock, silent, brooding, his eyes darting here and there, they said nothing for some of them also felt a strange and unpleasant presence to be there in their midst.

After weeks at sea Jack's ship was returning home and when they were once more in Mount's Bay, Jack, unhappy and restless as usual, evidently felt that he must talk and he confided to his mates that Sarah, on the scaffold, had made him promise on his oath that on that very day, at midnight, he would marry her. Thinking to comfort her in her last moments, he had agreed; but ever since that day she had never left him and, he added in a hollow voice . . . 'not being able to wed me in the flesh, she means to bind me to her forever in death.'

That night, at midnight, the ship's company in the immediate vicinity were awakened by the sound of footsteps, light and tripping, like someone in high heeled shoes. They traversed the passage leading to where Jack lay, unsleeping, in his hammock and without a word, his features contorted with terror, he rose and climbed on deck, the tap-tap-tap of the footsteps following close behind him.

On deck Jack did not hesitate: he made straight for the bulwark, clambered up and leapt deliberately and helplessly into the sea . . .

50

he was never seen again. As he disappeared some of his shipmates asserted that they heard the far-off chiming of church bells and many of them believed they were hearing Jack's wedding bells; Sarah had kept Jack to his word. Ever since, over the years, there have been reports of phantom wedding bells being heard, far out in Mount's Bay, and what sounds like a forlorn voice calling, 'I will . . . I will' before it is lost in the wind.

Mousehole

Amanda Casson told Marc Alexander, who has travelled extensively throughout Britain in his search for ghosts, that she had a curious and totally inexplicable experience at The Ship Inn when she was staying there in November, 1970.

**'There may be an unidentified ghost at
The Ship at Mousehole who occasionally appears.'**

She had just had a bath and on emerging from the bathroom, was walking down a long corridor when she saw the figure of a man leaning against the angle of the wall. He seemed to be wearing present-day clothes of grey cloth but as she approached him, he simply faded away and the corridor was deserted. There was no question of his moving: she actually watched as he grew less and less distinct until there was nothing where seconds earlier, there had been what appeared to be the solid and natural figure of a man.

Miss Casson, at that time manageress of an employment bureau in London, asked the proprietors of The Ship whether anyone else had ever seen such a figure or had reported anything odd, but no one seemed to know anything and there was, Miss Casson was told, no tradition of ghostly appearances at the inn.

Oddly enough my wife and I were having a drink at The Ship some years ago when we were staying at Marazion and we were chatting with another couple who were sharing our table, when the talk chanced to turn to ghosts. A local man who was standing nearby seemed to be interested in our conversation and after a few

'Trerice is a delightful house with a psychic fragrance and a gentle grey lady ghost.'

moments he came over and said he had once seen a ghost at The Ship.

It seemed that he had been helping the owner with some structural repairs in the upper part of the old inn one Sunday afternoon when the place was deserted and as he had walked along the upper corridor he had looked up to see a man walking ahead of him. The man appeared to be perfectly normal and there was certainly nothing frightening about the form until, as the local man was wondering to himself who on earth it could be, the figure was suddenly no longer there.

He thought he must have imagined the whole thing but it was so real and so natural and ordinary that he was very puzzled. He had mentioned the incident to the owner who had poured such scorn on his story that he had hardly mentioned the matter to anyone.

So it would seem that there may be an unidentified ghost man at The Ship who occasionally manifests for some unknown reason.

Newquay

Nearby Trerice, a property belonging to the National Trust but formerly owned, for over four centuries, by the Arundells, one of the great families of Cornwall, is a delightful house with a psychic fragrance and a gentle Grey Lady ghost.

A fascinating guide book to Newquay and the surrounding area, dating from the First World War, refers to Trerice as 'an ancient baronial mansion which the country people still declare to be haunted by the unhouseled spirit of a certain passionate Lord of Arundell, known in the neighbouring villages as "the wicked lord" . . . a delightful survival of the picturesque old days and the very ideal of an old haunted mansion . . . grey, venerable, hedged in with dark cypresses dotting the moss-grown lawn . . . The north wing of the old house was pulled down in the latter part of the nineteenth century, as no one would live in it, and all the personal possessions of the "wicked lord", his desk, papers, hunting and other gear, hurriedly burnt. For more than a century the place was left untouched . . .' And it is in the restored north wing that several psychic disturbances have been reported in recent years.

When I was last there in 1981 the north wing had only been open a few years and during alterations a number of unexplained happenings were reported. Doors opened by themselves; a 'presence' was distinctly felt by prosaic workmen; 'something' made a swishing sound along the old floorboards, reminiscent of someone passing by in crinolines. Then there is the mysterious 'whiff of perfume' and the occasional appearance of a Grey Lady who walks the north wing, along the Gallery and disappears down the stone circular stairway that once led to the original entrance to the house. Could all these happenings have any connection, one wonders, with the vague stories of the 'wicked lord' seducing a young servant girl and of her subsequent suicide?

One of the guides when I was there told me that she had noticed the 'inexplicable fragrance' (resembling lilac) on two occasions and several times she had had the distinct impression that someone or something had passed close by when no visible form was there. A former administrator of Trerice tells me there is a story of violent death at the house, fairly well substantiated, concerning a stable lad who was killed when some horses stampeded across the courtyard and his ghost had, repeatedly I am told, been seen in the area of the courtyard.

Many visitors to Trerice comment upon the atmosphere of the house; some have sensed the presence of death in the Library; some have felt that they have 'stepped back in time' when they have walked through the Gallery; one or two visitors have been so affected by the invisible influences in the Hall that they have left the house—but for the vast majority of the thousands of visitors who come to see beautiful Trerice every year, it is a place of peace and happiness, a welcome refuge for a while from the busy bustling world of the 1980s.

Padstow

Built about 1580 and lived in continuously ever since, The White Hart in Padstow is reputedly the oldest inn—although it is no longer a hostelry. Julie Frost, who moved into the premises with her husband Fred and two young sons in the 1950s, didn't give a second thought to vague stories of ghosts and ghostly happenings. The family soon acquired a dog, Crispin, and two cats, Bobo and Mister

Moses. Julie later described Crispin as 'a mixture of spaniel and retriever—a real tough guy', Bobo as 'every inch a lady, fastidious and gentle', and Moses as 'the bad lad of the trio—a spiv, and none too bright . . '

Nevertheless it was through the behaviour of their pets that the Frost family first became aware of peculiar happenings at The White Hart. Why, the whole family found themselves wondering, did Bobo sit in the window at dusk, eagerly looking out and seeing 'something' they couldn't see and welcoming 'it' with little chirruping sounds and purrs? She must be looking at the bats swooping about, they decided, but if this was so why did she run to the door and go walking round, tail erect, as if rubbing against the legs of a friend? And how was it that one day during a violent storm, when all the doors and windows were firmly closed and latched, did she arrive indoors, wet, before she could be admitted? And when a neighbourhood rogue cat pinned her down on a nearby roof, who pitched a stone so skilfully that her tormentor was sent flying?

Padstow harbour: At the White Hart there were 'vague stories of ghosts and ghostly happenings.'

Certainly no human being was in the area at the time.

Then there were footsteps. The heavy oak front door led into a passage and the vast iron bolt was always secured at dusk. Time after time all the family would hear footfalls pass the living room door and proceed upstairs. Once Julie was actually on the stairs when the footsteps began to approach with measured tread . . . she felt nothing. No sensation of coldness, no icy draught, no feeling of a 'presence', yet whatever it was must have passed at very close quarters, for the footsteps continued on up the stairs beyond her. In the bitter winter of 1963 Fred was the first member of the family to hear the strange breathing sound that soon became known as the 'iron lung'. It was a hollow, unpleasant, penetrating sound. Fred was in an upstairs room that first time and the sound seemed to emanate from a nearby bedroom; he walked quickly into the room—to be met by complete and utter silence.

The Frost family kept to themselves the strange happenings that they were experiencing and they never spoke of them to anyone outside the immediate family; but one day, out of the blue, a neighbour began to tell them about some historical research that he had been carrying out concerning his own house. In fact, he had learned little about his own property but he had discovered that many years earlier a priest, unable to find a bed at the nearby cleric's resthouse in St Edmund's Lane, had taken a bed at The White Hart. He had been an asthmatic and had fallen victim to a fearful attack during the night, and had died. The rasping noise that the occupants of The White Hart had so recently heard sounded just like someone having an asthmatic attack, they felt, and it was surely much more likely to be that than an iron lung.

The haunted family began to call their unbidden guest 'Wilfred' for no good reason but simply to put a name to it. Wilfred seemed to like milk bottles; on numerous occasions when the bottles were put out in the passage at night, 'he' would move them to the other side of the passage; not every night but it happened two or three times a month without fail.

And then there were the door movements. One fine summer evening when there was not a breath of wind, the heavy oak door, that had been closed but not bolted, opened by itself and gently swayed to and fro, creaking quietly. On and on it went until Fred Frost gently closed it and held it in position—and it shook and vibrated like a living thing beneath his hand. When Julie exchanged her hand for that of her husband's, it instantly became less active, ceased all movement and became what it was, still, dead wood.

Over the years there have been occupants of The White Hart who have neither heard nor felt anything unusual there; people perhaps who are not on the 'wavelength' that enables them to be in rapport with the supernormal, but when two old ladies, the Misses Reynolds, lived there, they were very much aware of odd happenings and especially of inexplicable footsteps. Times without number they would hear distinct footfalls in the front passage and sometimes they would look out but they never saw anything, or if they did they never said so, but they did hear footsteps—for which there was no possible explanation—mount the stairs and gradually fade away. They never heard the footsteps come down the stairs and they never felt that there was really anything to be frightened of although it was rather disturbing. They used to say they liked the house but not the noises the house made!

In 1964 the property was up for sale and another two ladies, this time a mother and daughter, came to view the place. Both were strangers to the district and neither knew anything about the house; yet as they were leaving the older woman said, with the conviction of years and in a tone that brooked no opposition: 'This place is haunted.' Another prospective buyer had left her shopping in one of the rooms while she looked round the rest of the empty house; when she returned she found that all her groceries had been removed from her bag and their individual wrappings and everything was arranged in a neat circle on the floor. She did not buy the property!

At that time the electrical system in the house left much to be desired; there were no such things as two-way switches and the last person to bed made their way upstairs in darkness, having switched off the downstairs light. One night Fred, who was usually the last to retire, arrived upstairs oddly shaken. He had switched off the light on the landing and had set off up the last short flight of stairs, as he had done scores of times before; at least he intended to do that but the moment the light was out he felt that he was lost although on thoroughly familiar ground and he described the sensation as feeling as though he was 'in a vacuum, a strange and timeless limbo'. There was complete loss of mental and physical orientation and a depth of darkness such as he had never known before that night. Although it sounds trivial, in fact the experience was distinctly

distasteful and distressing. Eventually he eased his way along the wall to the switch, having no idea how long he had been 'lost' or why he had not called out; but next day he bought the most powerful torch in Padstow and never went to bed again without it!

Some months later the Frost family heard with interest the experiences of a man who had once lived alone at The White Hart; an experience of a very similar nature but he apparently blundered into a furnished room and he described in some detail the contents and lay-out: in fact there was no such room or furniture in the house.

After the Frosts left The White Hart the house was temporarily empty and during this period some workmen, carrying out repairs, reported that they had distinctly seen the figures of two people in an upstairs room. Knowing that the house was empty and locked, they had taken steps to make sure that no one had broken in. Needless to say, no one had.

In relating some of the experiences of life at The White Hart thirty years ago, Mrs Frost told me in 1982 that she had not mentioned the few, but memorable, unpleasant happenings that she had never forgotten, adding: 'I loved that house, but now I am a widow and living alone, I don't think I would care to return . . .'

In September 1982 I explored the ancient Abbey House on North Quay; for the first time in its long history this quaint and sombre and mysterious house is open to the public. Abbey House is reputed to harbour a gentle ghost.

Prior to my visit I had talked with a long-standing resident of Padstow who told me she remembered hearing stories of the place being haunted when she was a girl. As a child she and her friends always passed Abbey House quietly, forever looking over their shoulders, and almost on tiptoe, in order not to disturb the ghost!

Abbey House is undoubtedly one of the oldest houses in Cornwall and records tell of it being an old house when Sir Walter Raleigh held his court on the South Quay during the reign of Queen Elizabeth I. Abbey House was the Guild House in the fifteenth century and the merchants of Padstow, who financed ventures from their busy port to Brittany and elsewhere, met there. Its name suggests an ecclesiastical connection but no one seems to know why

◄ **Abbey House, Padstow: 'Mrs Annie Simpson . . .**
became a familiar figure standing at the open gallery.'

the house is so named although, of course, Padstow was at one time a centre of Celtic Christianity. A thousand years ago the monastic community moved to Bodmin, following repeated raids by the warring Danes, but the monks retained an interest in Padstow, still owning much of the town, with the rest in the ownership of the Bishop. After Henry VIII dissolved the monasteries, Abbey House and much of Padstow was purchased by Nicholas Prideaux, Steward of the Prior of Bodmin, and the house remained the property of the Prideaux family until 1938 when it was bought by the eccentric Mrs Annie Simpson. I am told she was connected with the famous shoe firm but at all event she became a familiar figure, standing at the open gallery facing the harbour—and more than one inhabitant of Padstow expressed to me that conviction that they would not be at all surprised if she returned to haunt the house she lived in for more than forty years.

There were stories that she was always looking for the return of her lover, lost at sea, but in fact her husband was killed in a road accident soon after they moved to Abbey House and she lived on alone at the house on the quay until her death in 1981.

As I wandered through this building so full of memories, I learned that the ghost is thought to be that of a girl or young woman; an Elizabethan who climbs the fifteenth-century granite newel staircase from the age-old cellar, with its blocked-up tunnel running to Prideaux Place, and makes her silent way along the time-worn passage in the oldest part of this old house. Some people have detected a sense of loneliness and sadness in these parts of Abbey House, as though the girl is saying, 'nobody loves me . . . nobody cares about me . . .' The model of an Elizabethan girl, a red wax figure dating from about 1620 and exhibited in the house, is strangely evocative and could even represent I felt, the ghost of Abbey House.

Par

A ghost with a difference may haunt Daphne du Maurier's old home, the Rashleigh mansion, 'Menabilly', for she told my friend Joseph Braddock that a ghostly 'lady in blue' had been haunting the house since Edwardian times; a gentle, quiet, harmless figure that was only ever seen looking out of a certain bedroom window. The famous author of haunting *Rebecca, Jamaica Inn, Vanishing Cornwall* and so many other wonderful books, made extensive enquiries over a long period but she was never able to definitely establish who this 'lady in blue' might be and then a novel thought struck her. Could the ghost be not a phantom from the past but a peep into the future? When Daphne du Maurier came to write *The King's General*, she wrote it in the room where the ghostly lady was reputed to appear and, as she worked, the authoress would herself rest from time to time and look out of that very window for inspiration, and she invariably wore her blue working smock! It amused her to think that those who had said they had seen the 'lady in blue' as they walked across the sweeping lawns in 1910 and over the succeeding years might have seen, not a ghost from the past, but herself in 1945!

Penryn

Just before Christmas a phantom coach and horses is said to drive through this town: some people say the horses are headless, some say the driver has no head, and some say the story dates back to the days of smuggling . . . but why only once a year, a few days before Christmas?

Another ghost was immortalized here in a melodrama entitled 'The Penryn Tragedy'. The story goes that after long years at sea a sailor returned to his native town to see his old parents who ran an inn. For a joke the returning son thought he would fool the old people for a while and he disguised himself and booked a room at the inn, where he was taken for a rich man who had come to Penryn by accident and was known to no one and no one knew that he was there. In fact he had confided his idea of a joke to his sister who lived in another part of Penryn.

The innkeeper and his wife decided to murder their unknown guest while he was the worse for drink, to gain possession of the money they believed he carried with him. Only after they had committed the crime did they recognize the dead man as their son.

The shock and horror at what they had done caused them both to commit suicide and their daughter died of a broken heart soon afterwards. For years the place was reported to be unquiet at dead of night; heavy thumps and bangs sounding in the stillness, strange whisperings being borne away on the night air and terrifying sighs and groans disturbing the quiet of night and echoing in the darkness.

Penzance

'Oh yes, we've got a ghost here alright' my wife and I were told when we called at The Dolphin Inn, one of Cornwall's oldest inns; 'in fact two ghosts . . .'

The best-known ghost visitor is thought to be an old sea captain who died here and those who claim to have seen the ghost form describe it as a swarthy figure wearing a tricorn hat, lace ruffles and with brass buttons on his coat. A previous landlord's wife saw 'the Captain' or 'George' as he is variously called, several times and it is not unknown for a visitor, without knowing anything about the reputed ghost, to ask about the formidable old sea-dog they thought they caught a glimpse of. More frequently they will ask about the ghostly footsteps which have been heard many times by reputable witnesses.

Both the present landlord and his wife have heard the heavy, measured tread, marching across the ceiling and sometimes continuing down the stairs. It always seems to begin in the front and original upper part of the inn, pass over the bar and disappear towards the back of the building. At the rear of the inn's main cellar, there is an open space, rather like the bottom of a lift shaft and here in 1873 a young man was killed in an unfortunate accident and his phantom form is reputed to be the second ghost at The Dolphin.

Within the last few years the figure of a young man with fair hair has also been seen in one of the bedrooms; Mary Clark saw him twice in one week; but it is not known whether he or 'the Captain' is responsible for another psychic manifestation here.

In Room 4 a mysterious depression is often noticed in a cushion that rests on a certain chair, exactly as though someone has just been sitting there and no matter how often the cushion is shaken up and replaced, even when the room is unused and locked, the indentation always reappears. Next door, in Room 5, a somewhat similar indentation has been seen in the bed and pillow, almost as though someone invisible is sleeping or resting there.

From time to time other odd things have been noticed at the inn: traces of the old-fashioned coarse tobacco; a dragging noise and the sound of whispering from empty rooms. Sir John Hawkins set up his headquarters here in 1588 when he was enlisting Cornishmen to fight the Spanish Armada and there must have been many whispered conversations in those turbulent days. Some years ago a secret hiding place was discovered still containing two casks of rum and there is little doubt that The Dolphin was once a smugglers' inn; there must have been many times when a dragging noise was heard here at dead of night in those days. Judge Jeffreys held court here in what is now the dining room, while the prisoners were kept in the cellars so it may be from those far off days that the dragging noise originated. As for the old-fashioned tobacco, well, it is said that Sir

**The Dolphin Inn, Penzance: 'We've got a ghost
here alright . . . in fact two ghosts.'**

Walter Raleigh enjoyed the first pipe of tobacco to be smoked in England at The Dolphin!

Chapel Street is reputed to be haunted by the ghost of old Mrs Baines who was mistaken for a thief and shot. Her figure is said to be seen on occasions, wearing a dark cloak and bonnet, at the top of the street and disappearing into a wall.

An old house in Morrab Road, once a doctors' surgery and later an old peoples' home, has long been said to be haunted. During the latter period a number of curious happenings were reported including the shadowy form of a man standing beside a bedroom window. This unidentified ghost was seen by several members of the staff of the home and also by patients and visitors. He is thought to be the ghost of a dead doctor who was so dedicated to his patients that even death cannot give him rest; possibly he is the first resident doctor at the home—certainly the sightings date from his death.

Fairly recently two girl babysitters, knowing nothing of the history of the house or the reputed ghost, saw a man walk along the hall and disappear into the room that once served as a surgery. They investigated immediately but found the room completely deserted. Later that night they again both saw the same figure traverse the same area and afterwards they refused to babysit in the house; a very understandable decision.

Perranporth

A wooden cabin on a caravan site here was reported to be haunted by several occupants and by the camp owner.

Peter Moss recounts the experience of two ladies who were disturbed at night by the sound of stealthy footsteps padding round the outside of the building, although they saw nothing. Suddenly the front door, which they had been careful to close and lock, burst open and then slammed shut, all of its own accord; and then the padding sounds seemed to emanate from inside the cabin, in fact from the living room next door to the bedroom occupied by the two frightened ladies! One of them called out 'Who the devil are you?' and this produced a sudden and complete silence.

Moments later they heard the sound of rustling papers and a quiet chuckle, as though someone was enjoying what they were reading.

The rustle and crinkle of paper was then heard again, followed by another chuckle and then a noise that sounded like something breaking. Plucking up their courage the two puzzled visitors looked at each other and then got out of their beds and threw open the door—the living room was completely deserted but a rocking chair was swaying to and fro as though someone was seated in it; the steady rhythm continued and again they both heard a chuckle and the rustle of invisible paper. As they went into the room they seemed to sense the low growl of an unseen animal, situated somewhere behind the still moving rocking chair. The two ladies had had enough. They fled back to their bedroom and remained huddled together until dawn. At first light they packed their cases and set out to see the camp owner who told them she was not surprised for she had heard similar reports from other visitors. She offered the two ladies the use of a luxury caravan for the rest of their stay and there they passed peaceful and uneventful days and nights.

Perranzabuloe

A ghost story that smacks of a dream caused by a guilty conscience is told of an old woman who found a set of false teeth protruding from the soil in Perranzabuloe churchyard. Thinking she might find a use for them, she picked them up, took them home and placed them in her bedroom.

That night she always said she was awakened from her sleep by noises outside her cottage window and a spectral voice demanded, over and over again: 'Give me back my teeth! Give me back my teeth!' Hastily snatching up the wretched teeth, the old woman flung them out of the window, without daring to look at whatever might be there, but when the teeth left her hand, the noises and the voice ceased and she heard footsteps going away from the house in the direction of the churchyard.

Next morning, before anyone was about, she searched the soft ground outside her window and the muddy roadway but of the teeth there was no sign; nor were there any footprints or any marks that might account for the sounds that she had heard during the night.

As folklorist Christina Hole said to me as she told me this story: 'The old woman never heard the voice or the footsteps again, nor, I

A woman found a set of false teeth in Perranzabuloe churchyard.

imagine, did she ever again bring back any finds from the churchyard!'

Polperro

A correspondent tells me that he heard two men talking about a smuggler's ghost that haunted the caves here. There is a story that two fair-traders fell out over the sharing of some gold and in the fight that followed, one of them was killed. Thereafter his ghost haunted the cave, looking for his fair share of the gold that belonged to neither of them.

Certainly there are persistent reports of a dark form being seen in the caves by local people and visitors alike. One of the phantoms that is reputed to wander among the maze of tunnels behind the

A smuggler's ghost haunted the caves at Polperro.

cavern below Chapel Hill on the west side of the harbour is thought
to be of Willy Willock. He was a fisherman who set out to explore
the subterranean labyrinth and was never seen again. His ghost is
reported to be seen and heard on dark and quiet nights, his ghostly
cries, the shrieks of a dying man, issuing from the mouth of the cave
where he starved to death, within a stone's throw of the cave
entrance.

Porthtowan

On that part of the road to Portreath known as Mile Hill, stands
the strangely named Dog and Dragon, a restaurant of distinction.
    The story behind the name is that many, many years ago the
neighbourhood hereabouts was greatly troubled by a fire-breathing

67

dragon that regularly stole and ate sheep and cattle. One May Eve, once a great festival for the return of life and virility, just before midnight, the dragon was met by a huge white, spotted dog that growled a warning. As the dragon went for the nearest sheep, the dog sank its teeth into the hind-quarters of the dragon and the fight was on. The dragon tried to catch the dog as the dog snapped again and again at the dragon's tail and round and round they flew, the dragon becoming more and more angry and confused until the sun began to rise and the dog, with sudden determination, tore off the tip of the dragon's tail. The monster gave a terrible howl of pain and disappeared in the direction of the sea and was never seen again. An ancient 'dragon-path' or 'ley' runs through the lands where the Dog and Dragon now stands—but all this can surely have no connection with the mysterious spectral dog that has been seen hereabouts from time to time? Oddly enough most of the sightings correspond with the festival nights of the old Celtic calendar: Midsummer, Midwinter, Beltane, Hallowe'en, Candlemas Day and Lammas-tide but most frequently, it seems, on May Eve.

Portreath

When I was here a year or two ago I was told about a phantom-man who occasionally appeared in the vicinity of a corner seat of the restaurant that stands on the site of a large old stone building that in recent years had been used for storing fishing and boating tackle. In former years, however, it had been used, not infrequently as a temporary morgue for the many unidentified and unclaimed bodies that were always being washed ashore during gales. Any unclaimed bodies were laid to rest with a headstone bearing the date and such words as 'unknown sailor'. It is thought that the still figure seen at Portreath has the air of waiting for someone, perhaps for some loved one, to come and claim his body for burial.

The Smugglers Cottage Guest House, on West Beach, has long been considered to be haunted. Some thirty years ago a small secret

◀'The dragon tried to catch the dog as the dog snapped again and again at the dragon's tail.'

closet was uncovered during the course of alterations, a closet that contained a small table, the skeleton of a man and the remains of his black cloak, an ancient sea chest and an old sword. The sword and the table were presented to the Exeter Museum.

Whether the skeleton has any connection with the ghost of the slight young man, dressed in what has been described as 'Jacobean style', is not known, but the discovery of the human remains made no difference to the appearances of the ghost which is usually described as appearing out of the wall panelling in a corridor on the first floor and walking 'furtively' towards the stairs, where 'he' vanishes. The place where the ghost appears is said to be the original entrance to a tunnel leading down to the beach.

The ghost was reportedly seen by two nurses and a dog on one occasion, and ten years later by a visitor who thought a fancy-dress dance must be taking place somewhere in the vicinity. A few years earlier a party of ghost-hunters spent four hours of darkness and discomfort in the haunted passage and were rewarded by a sudden drop in the temperature at 1.30 a.m. and at the same time a dog, accompanying the watchers, seemed to sense something invisible to its human companions.

Poundstock

Beautiful Penfound Manor has been the scene of apparently ghostly manifestations, which have usually been associated with Kate Penfound who lived here during the Civil War.

Kate was in love with John Trebarfoot of nearby Trebarfoot Manor but he and his family supported Cromwell while the Penfounds were Royalists. When neither Kate nor John could convince their respective families that love was more important than politics, the young couple decided to elope and one April evening, traditionally the 26th, Kate made her way through the window of her bedroom into the arms of her waiting lover but Arthur Penfound, Kate's father, suddenly faced the couple in the courtyard

'Kate's white face has been reportedly seen peering from her bedroom window.' ▶

**St Neot Church, Poundstock is reputed to be
haunted by the ghost of a murdered priest . . .**

and in the fight that followed both Kate and John died. Some say
that Penfound in his blind anger shot both his daughter and her
lover; others say that in attempting to come between John and her
father, Kate was shot and the men fought on and killed each other.
At all events each April 26th the ghost of Kate Penfound is said to
appear and rejoin her lover John in the courtyard and at other times
her father has been seen in various parts of this utterly charming
and atmospheric house. Sometimes Kate's white face has reportedly
been seen, peering from the window in her bedroom, looking for her
lover, as she must have looked three hundred years ago, little
thinking they would both be dead, by the arm of her father, within
an hour or so.

Previous occupants of Penfound Manor asserted they sometimes
heard distinct voices; and the son of a former tenant maintains that
he saw the ghostly form of Kate on several occasions, crossing the
Great Hall on her way towards the main stairs. The present

. . . to this day, it is said, he can be
seen, wandering among the graves and inside the church.

residents have had no sightings of the ghosts and no manifestations
of any kind in recent years, although when they first went there
they were occasionally disturbed by the sound of voices and odd
bangs and crashing sounds coming from the direction of Kate's
bedroom and the courtyard below, which must be much as it was
when two people who passionately loved one another, died there.

The church of St Neot at Poundstock is reputed to be haunted by
the ghost of a murdered priest. William Penfound was celebrating
Mass in December, 1356, when several parishioners entered the
church and, for some unknown reason, murdered the priest. The two
ringleaders, named as John Bevill and Simon de St Gennys, were
arrested and stood trial but were pardoned—one cannot help
pondering on the story that must lie behind the deed and the
pardon. No wonder that to this day the ghostly form of the
Reverend William Penfound is said to sometimes be seen, wandering among the graves and inside the church he loved.

Praa Sands

Pengersick Castle was once occupied by the violent Henry de Pengersick, known as Henry la Fort, who was excommunicated for attacking and wounding a vicar and a monk, among his other virtues. The present occupants tell me: 'If ghost there is, we would be inclined to think that it is that of Henry la Fort . . .'

Several very ancient legends are associated with Pengersick involving magic swords, witches, a magic white hare and the elixir of life. In later days, John Milliton, who rebuilt the place as a fortified manor, is thought by some people to haunt the house where he tried to murder his wife with poisoned wine, but she craftily changed goblets. Another story is that, while they were dining together, Milliton suddenly announced that he had poisoned his wife's drink: whereupon she replied that in that case they would both die, for she had poisoned his! Of such activities ghosts are born.

Some visitors do feel an unaccountable 'presence' at Pengersick but such elusive ghosts as there may be here do not disturb in any way the present occupants or their pets, three cats and a dog.

Roche Rock

A ruined fifteenth-century chapel, set high among this rocky outcrop, is reputed to be haunted by the ghost of a man who sometimes stares angrily from his lofty perch and certainly many visitors to this strange spot have reported seeing a shadowy figure moving among the rocks. At first they have thought a real person is up there casting a shadow and then they have realised that the 'shadow' can be seen in different positions and from different directions and that it resembles a man, bent over and hurrying about the rocks.

Some people say the ghost is that of a miner, others that he was a leper, others again—since this is Cornwall—that he was a smuggler.

◀'Pengersick Castle once occupied by the violent Henry la Fort who was excommunicated for attacking and wounding a vicar . . .'

A few visitors to this isolated place have remarked upon strange sounds that they have heard apparently emanating from the chapel ruin.

St Germans

The good St German, it is said, came to Cornwall in the reign of the free-thinking orthodox Catholic Roman Emperor Valentinian, but his doctrines of freewill and the value of good works and his many remarkable miracles met stiff opposition and he was persecuted by some of the priests and monks and many of the local people.

One Sunday, while attending to his pious duties, a brawl developed and he was set upon. Eventually he escaped and fled to a lonely place where he prayed for his persecutors. So intense was the agony and soul-suffering of this holy man that it is recorded that the very rocks felt the power of his sadness 'and wept with him', and the

Port Eliot, St Germans: '. . . during a children's party the ghost monk was seen by many of them.'

weeping rocks were known as the Well of St German.

The parish has associations with early Christianity in Britain and was the original seat of the Cornish bishopric. It was the see of Bishop Burhwold who died in 1027 and Bishop Leofric founded a priory here.

Has the ghost monk that has long haunted the area walked for more than nine centuries? Certainly there are many stories and accounts of a ghost monk being encountered at St Germans and in October, 1982, a former resident told me that the ghost was well-known in the vicinity and had been encountered by many people; a lonely, pathetic, harmless figure that was often taken for a real monk but sometimes it was recognized as a ghost, especially, it seems, by children. My informant told me that a few years ago during a party for children at Port Eliot, the medieval and embattled mansion next to the Abbey Church, the ghost monk put in an appearance and was seen by some of the adults and by many of the children. The party was abandonded.

St Ives

Elliott O'Donnell once told me of a new house he rented for a time here when he was repeatedly disturbed at night by the sound of clinking footsteps that halted outside his door. Then he would hear a loud knock on the top panel of the door, followed by complete silence. Time after time O'Donnell would throw open the door but he never saw anything. Invariably all sounds would cease as soon as he opened the door, but there could be no doubt about the distinctive tap of approaching footsteps, suggesting a person wearing high-heeled shoes, and the sharp knock on the upper part of the bedroom door. The other disturbances, reported by O'Donnell and by later occupants, were the sound of doors opening and closing at dead of night and of footsteps mounting the stairs, but they were never heard descending.

One night O'Donnell sprinkled the passage outside his bedroom door with flour and sand alternately, and he fixed a line of cotton, breast-high across the passage but the footsteps came that night as before and the cotton was unbroken and the flour and sand showed no sign of any disturbance. Several housekeepers employed by

O'Donnell left because of the disturbances. Elliott O'Donnell, a keen student himself of all aspects of psychic phenomena, believed that the land on which the house had been built attracted elementals and that they subsequently manifested inside the house.

The famous bay of St Ives has long been said to be haunted by phantom bells. There is also reputed to be a ghost ship that appears in the bay from time to time firing distress rockets, but when the would-be rescuers manage to get almost alongside the old-fashioned ship, it suddenly vanishes. Another story is told here of a ship in distress in the bay, a real ship this time, the *Neptune* out of London, but by the time the local men reached the spot, the vessel had sunk beneath the waves—in the very place where the phantom ship had vanished.

Among the many unfortunate ships wrecked off the coast here one carried a passenger who, as the ship went down, clasped her baby and leapt for the safety of the lifeboats but the heavy seas swept the child from her arms and away into the darkness of the sea and storm.

The mother was pulled out of the sea, more dead than alive, but she never recovered from the tragic loss of her baby. At her funeral some of the mourning folk of St Ives said they saw the figure of a woman float away from the grave towards the open sea. For many years there have been stories of the sad figure of a woman searching for her baby along the shore here on dark and stormy nights; a figure that disappears seawards whenever it is approached.

St Just

An inn in the Pendeen-Botallack area was and perhaps still is haunted on the anniversary of a fight to the death. My informant's grandfather lodged at the inn around the turn of the century and he was in the habit of sitting and reading or having a chat with the landlord in the evenings, after work.

One night the landlord suggested that he might like to go for a

The ghost ship of St Ives appears firing distress rockets but vanishes as the rescuers come alongside. ▶

walk but after a hard day's work the lodger felt tired and put his feet up instead. He sensed that the landlord grew more and more uneasy and then suddenly without any warning, there was a tremendous thumping noise from the room above and the sound of fighting, the beams moving and shuddering under the violent movements; then all of a sudden the door of an upstairs room burst open followed by the sound of a man falling heavily down the stairs—then silence.

The lodger, alarmed and puzzled, rose to his feet to see what was afoot but the landlord restrained him, saying there was nothing he could do and there were to be no more disturbances. Apparently many years earlier two brothers had fought savagely in the room above and one had been killed and each year on the anniversary of the event the sound of the struggle was heard and the floorboards were seen to strain and move as long as the fight persisted, but after the sound of the losing combatant falling down the stairs, all was quiet until the following year. Feeling that he would lose lodgers if it was known that the house was haunted, the landlord had always tried to persuade his lodgers to be out of the house on the night of the anniversary and he usually succeeded. My informant told me that her grandfather had lived to a great age; she remembered hearing of the ghostly fight when she was very young. He always told the same story of the events of that night which remained a vivid and lasting memory for the rest of his life.

St Levan

A ghostly bell that seems to emanate from a sea captain's grave here is said to foretell the death of anyone unfortunate enough to hear it and there is a ghostly woman in a white garment also haunting the churchyard.

The haunted grave is that of Captain Richard Wetherall who perished when his brig, *Aurora*, sank in December 1811, and it is said that a seafaring man will hear the muffled sound of eight bells, signifying that his life's 'watch' will soon be over.

The ghostly woman in white walks on summer evenings and dates back several centuries but is still seen occasionally, I am told, but who she is and why she walks I have been unable to discover.

Doubtless some of the reported sightings of this ghost have a natural explanation but at least one encounter that was related to me firsthand seems quite impossible to explain away in rational terms.

Sennen

Nearby Penrose, now a farmhouse, was once the home of a family of that name. Some three hundred years ago seafaring Ralph Penrose was broken-hearted when his wife died of a fever and more and more he left Penrose in the care of his brother John and went to sea, taking with him his seven-year-old son and his cousin William.

One night their ship ran into a storm and foundered in sight of home. Flares warned John and other local people what was happening but, on John's instructions, they stood and watched and

Penrose Farm near Sennen

did nothing to help. Only the boy, true heir to Penrose, survived it seemed and he was washed up on the shore—only to be murdered by John Penrose who then took over the house and the lands as his own.

Unknown to anyone William, too, had survived but with no memory of anything before the shipwreck, and he wandered far and wide until one day, quite by chance, he turned up at Penrose and heard the boy's voice which said: 'My uncle murdered me . . . I lie beneath the dead tree in the orchard . . . avenge the murder of your cousin's son . . . dig, and give me peace . . .'

William sought out a trusted friend and together they unearthed the remains of the murdered boy. They carried the remains by night to Sennen churchyard and there buried what was left of the little body.

Back at Penrose they found the body of John, hanging from a beam. He had hanged himself in sight of the disturbed grave of the innocent boy he had murdered.

William settled for a time at Penrose but before long he found the place to be so haunted that he gave up his rights to it and went away forever.

Sennen Cove is haunted by a ghost known as 'the Irish lady'. The story goes that she was the sole survivor of an Irish ship which foundered here. She managed to swim to a rock and haul herself to safety—or so she thought, but the sea was so rough that it was impossible to rescue her and for several days and nights people on shore watched helplessly as she waved imploringly at them to save her; eventually she died from thirst, hunger and exposure and the waves washed her body back into the sea. Ever since, when the waves run high at Sennen Cove, the ghostly form of 'the Irish lady' is seen clinging desperately to the rock that now bears her name.

Sennen Cove has also long been reputed to be haunted by phantom bells. Stanley Baron is just one witness who has told me of the eerie sound that has been heard by many people over the years. Stanley was staying with a local family and one night, just after eleven o'clock, having composed one of his articles for the national daily to which he regularly contributed, he went to bed. But not to

◀Lyonesse: '. . . driving towards Land's End . . .
she saw those towers and spires and domes far out to sea.'

sleep; he seemed to toss and turn all night, he said possibly because he was over-tired but the sea-sprayed sands of the bay were a stone's throw from his window and, about one o'clock he began to realize that in addition to the usual sounds of the sea there was a rhythmic clanging of bells. All this continued until about three o'clock, when he fell into a deep sleep.

At four o'clock, as he saw from his bedside clock, he was awakened by the long, low pealing of distant and muffled bells. Gradually their chiming diminished with the coming of the dawn.

At breakfast Stanley asked his hosts whether they had been awakened during the night by the sound of bells. 'They must have been the Lost Land Bells you heard . . .' he was told. Of course, he thought, the Lost Land, the Drowned Land of Lyonesse, with its seven score churches; drowned according to Cornish tradition, in two mighty surges of ocean, one in 1014 and the other in 1094.

Miss Edith Oliver, former Mayor of Wilton and author of the Preface to the first edition of the famous *An Adventure* in which the real names of the authors appeared, heard no phantom bells but saw, far out at sea, from Land's End, what she afterwards thought must have been a vision of lost Lyonesse.

Miss Oliver was making her first visit to Land's End and on a beautiful bright day she stood on the edge of the cliffs, looking out at the vastness of the sea. As she stared, she saw, to her utter astonishment but with a clarity only dimmed by distance, what appeared to be a town of some importance, seemingly some miles out at sea: a jumble of towers, domes, spires and battlements. Thinking she must be seeing the Scilly Isles she was still looking at the distant domes and towers when a coastguard approached her. She promptly asked him the name of the town she could see, to which he replied: 'There's no town there; only the sea . . .'

When she looked back, there was no sign of the town she had been looking at for several moments but, when she began to make enquiries, she discovered that others had had a similar experience: seeing, from the precipitous coast of Land's End, what they believed to be part of lost Lyonesse.

A year or two later she had another visionary glimpse of the phantom city. She was driving towards Land's End, accompanied by a friend, Miss MacPherson, one wet and blustery evening, when she again saw those towers and spires and domes, standing immovable far out to sea. 'Do you see anything over there?' she asked her friend. 'Indeed, I do', replied Miss MacPherson, 'I see a city! I've often been told that from here it is possible to catch sight of the lost city of Lyonesse, but I've never seen it before . . .' Some years later Miss MacPherson saw the visionary city again when she was accompanied by her sister, who could see nothing.

Stratton

The lands of nearby Binhamy Farm include all that remains of haunted Blanchminster Castle. With the permission of the present owner, after crossing a couple of fields, you reach the site of the Crusader, Sir Ranulph de Blanchminster's stronghold.

When he returned from his holy campaign and discovered that his wife had given him up for dead and married another, Sir Ranulph became a recluse although, as lord of the manor, he was always a great benefactor to Stratton, the small market town mentioned in the Domesday Book that was probably a Roman station. His damaged effigy is to be seen in the fourteenth-century church but the sad and lonely form of his ghost has also been seen near the still discernible moat of his once-great castle. I talked with a man in 1982 who minutely described the armoured and chain-mailed figure that passed a foot or so above the level of the present ground, until silently, and with an air of inconsolable grief, it melted into nothingness in front of his unbelieving eyes.

Tintagel

Legend has it that King Arthur was conceived and born here but if he was he had no connection with the present crumbling castle that was not built until six or seven hundred years after his death—but perhaps there was an earlier castle—perhaps . . . perhaps . . . At all events there have been reported glimpses of the ghostly figure of the great King among these dark ruins and certainly the atmosphere is conducive to such experiences; the aura of mystery that has surrounded Tintagel for centuries has not yet disappeared.

That there is a strange and mystic influence hereabouts is evident from the number of people who believed that they have seen or sensed something of the past among these black cliffs and crumbling ruins where, even on the sunniest days, there is a sombre stillness, broken only by the sound of the ever-roaring sea.

The ruined castle, once a year, is thought by some people to disappear and re-appear in all its former glory, before returning to its present condition. Barras Head, the headland north of the castle, has a reputation for many strange happenings; dogs in particular often seem to sense something strange and invisible to their human companions. 'There is,' as one resident put it to me, 'something very odd about Barras Head.'

Torpoint

Some years ago my friend John Butler, the Baker Street dentist, visited Antony House before it passed into the care of the National Trust. He and a friend were exploring Cornwall, without a map or guide book, going wherever their fancy took them. They came across this impressive house which they began to wander round without a guide and they started to climb the enormous stairway with its Corinthian columns and bubble lights—blown glass globes of the Queen Anne period. When they were almost at the top of the stairs, facing the green room, John came to a sudden halt and said he could not go on. He saw nothing but had the overwhelming impression that he was not welcome and should not continue his tour of the house.

Puzzled, for it was a feeling he had never previously experienced, he tried to go on but the feeling became so strong that he turned back, left the house and never did visit the upper rooms.

Years later, John Butler's nurse visited Antony House and in a guide book she discovered that a previous occupant of the house had borne the name Butler!

In 1901 Reginald Carew Pole, aide-de-camp to Lord Roberts in the Afghan War, married Lady Beatrice Butler, daughter of the 3rd

Tintagel: 'There have been reported glimpses of the ghostly figure of the great king among the ruins . . .' ▶

Marquess of Ormond. John always wondered whether something had happened at Antony House to someone bearing his name that had left behind an intangible 'something' that he had encountered. Antony House was the scene of a remarkable and well-attested ghost story. In October 1880 Lady Helen Waldegrave visited the Carew Pole family, taking with her Helen Alexander, her Scottish maid, who was taken ill shortly after their arrival. When the local doctor diagnosed typhoid fever one of the housemaids, Frances Reddel, was detailed to serve as night nurse to the ailing girl.

One night the temporary nurse, a very capable and stolid girl, was preparing a dose of medicine when she saw a large, elderly lady enter the bedroom and walk towards the bed. There had been no knock on the door and noticing the visitor was dressed in a long, red nightgown over a red flannel petticoat—with a hole in it, evidently caused by stay busks!—Frances decided that the ill girl's mother must have been sent for. She watched as the figure, carrying an ornate brass candlestick, approached the restive patient, sat on the bed, and looked earnestly at the ill girl. Frances then turned back to her task of preparing the medicine.

A moment later, the medicine ready, she turned and approached the bed to find, to her amazement, that there was no sign of the stout lady she had so plainly seen seconds earlier! However the condition of the patient soon put all other thoughts out of her mind. The poor girl was obviously very ill and Frances hurriedly summoned the doctor but Helen Alexander was beyond human aid and within two hours she was dead.

Two days later the dead girl's family arrived from Scotland and when Frances saw Helen's mother, she almost fainted with shock. In every physical respect this stout, elderly, motherly figure resembled the form she had seen visiting her dying patient two days earlier at four o'clock in the morning! Later, after the funeral, Frances mentioned the incident to Helen's sister who immediately remarked that her mother habitually wore a red nightgown and that she possessed a red flannel petticoat—with a hole in it which the busks of her stays had worn through the material! Furthermore her mother possessed an ornate brass candlestick, such as Frances described.

It was established that neither Helen nor anyone else had written to Helen's parents about the girl being ill for she was fully convinced that she would soon be fit and well again, yet on the evening of her death, her mother had suddenly said to her husband: 'I'm worried about Helen. I have a feeling she is very ill . . .' No explanation has ever been forthcoming for one of the strangest stories ever to come out of Cornwall but one possibility is that the figure Frances saw was projected in some way which we do not yet understand from the mind of the dying girl.

Tregeseal

On the outskirts of St Just, Chyoone Farmhouse has been the scene of phantom hoofbeats and the rumble of an unseen coach. Mrs Ethel Waters told Michael Williams that she had heard the sounds 'at least a dozen times, maybe twenty times . . .' They were heard coming down the road, perhaps two or three hundred yards away, as if they were turning off the main road and they always halted at the farm.

One theory to account for the sounds is that a toll house once stood on the site of Chyoone Farmhouse and that the track of the phantom coach and horses follows a turnpike road.

Truro

Here there are at least two haunted inns: The Star in Castle Street where, long ago, a girl was murdered and her form has been glimpsed by sober witnesses, especially in the late evening; and The William the Fourth in Kenwyn Street, reputedly built on the site of a Dominican friary, an oft-repeated snippet of local history that coincides with the ghostly figure of a friar that has been seen hereabouts from time to time.

A field on the outskirts of the town, known as Comprigney, takes its name from the Cornish, 'the field of the gibbet', which it probably once was and there are local people to this day who avoid the area after dark because of 'shadowy figures' that have been seen and 'rattling chains' that have been heard: visual and audible echoes perhaps from the past . . .

Veryan

A sixteenth-century house here, once known as Crugsillick Manor, was built by the Kempe family and it remained in their possession for over three hundred years. One member of the family, Admiral Kempe, a seafarer who had sailed with Captain Cook, seems to return to the house from time to time when he is seen by some people and not others.

In September 1982 I talked with Bill Pilgrim. During the twelve years, prior to 1978, that he and his wife lived at the house, they became completely convinced of the haunting of the place by Admiral Kempe. They never saw anything themselves although they were present on each occasion when they can vouch for the fact that other people said they saw the figure. None of those who saw the ghost had any knowledge of the place being haunted, of a ghost having been seen there or anything about Admiral Kempe; yet they all minutely described the same figure. All the four known sightings took place within a period of five years; the figure was always seen in the evening, between seven and nine o'clock, and it always seemed to materialize at the same place on the ground floor and remain within a restrictive area. Many people sensed that there was something odd about this part of the house, without seeing the ghost or knowing anything about it.

All the people who saw the ghost said he had a smile on his face and he certainly never frightened anyone. The general description included grey hair, a long plain coat of some dark material with brass buttons down the front, and strangely square hands. The uniform is thought to be a sort of undress uniform coat worn by officers of the day.

Once, in the middle of the dining room, a guest felt a heavy hand rest on his shoulder and wondering who it could be, he turned quickly round, to find the dining room deserted. The wife of his friend, sitting opposite, was even more amazed, for she had seen the ghostly Admiral lay his hand on her friend's shoulder, before vanishing as he turned round.

The house has changed hands many times over the years, each occupant making structural alterations to the place, but the ghost of Admiral Kempe seems to return every so often, irrespective of the environment or the occupants. He has been doing so for centuries, according to local people who told the Pilgrims, when they asked about any reputed ghost, that the place had been haunted for years by the ghost of the restless Admiral Kempe.

The church clock is said to be a harbinger of death in the village if it strikes on a Sunday morning during certain parts of the service for then a member of the parish will surely die before the following Sunday. There are several round houses in Veryan, supposedly built in such a way that the Devil could find no corner to hide.

Wadebridge

Each New Year's Eve, at midnight, a phantom coach, drawn by four horses and driven by a headless coachman, is said to gallop through the courtyard of the Molesworth Arms Hotel and out of the hallway . . . there are some people who claim to have seen and heard it, I have been told; other people hear it only and see nothing; others again hear and see nothing but feel its presence unmistakably . . .

The Molesworth Arms in Molesworth Street is one of the old original coaching inns, more than four hundred years old and so named because at one time it was owned by the prominent Molesworth family who were the principal landowners in the area. Today the crest of this distinguished family can still be seen high over the main entrance to the hotel.

Another cyclic ghost is reputed to visit Trewornan Bridge where, once a year, on a night of the full moon, a phantom coach and horses races across one of the oldest bridges in Cornwall.

The delightful cottage 'Treneague' beside a little brook known as Hay Stream, has long been haunted, in a fittingly quiet and peaceful way, by three ghostly monks. They have been seen sitting on a bench in one of the rooms, drinking ghostly beer; and this appearance seems plausible for the charming house, where my wife and I stayed when James and Catherine Turner lived there, is said to have once belonged to the monastery at Pawton, a mile or so away, and to have been one of its out-farms. I found the place utterly peaceful and unhaunted by any troublesome ghost although I did do an oil painting of the place and included three ghostly monks! And I am sure the present occupants find the atmosphere equally idyllic.

Yet ghosts there are in this part of Cornwall. Listen to Arthur Norway, writing in 1922, for his *Highways and Byways in Devon and Cornwall:* 'This valley of the river Camel is full of haunted lanes and houses. A mile or so up the river stands the ancient church of Egloshayle . . . here you might see—but never save when the moon is bright—a white rabbit gambolling about the open space beside the churchyard wall; a pretty, long-eared rabbit with pink eyes . . . it goes loppeting about among the grasses . . . and if anyone should pass, will sit and look at him with fearless eyes. And well it might. It has nothing to dread from anyone dwelling in these parts . . .' It seems that it is a ghost animal and there are stories of people taking a stick to it in the past but blows have no effect on ghosts and it is the sticks that have broken, 'as if they had struck a rock'. We are told that no one knows the history of the rabbit but it has been reported for generations.

There is a story too of a man who said he would put an end to the rabbit and he took a gun to it one night. Some of his companions followed at a distance and soon heard a gun fired and a loud cry . . . they ran to the place where the ghost rabbit always appeared but neither rabbit nor sportsman was to be seen. At last they found the man, lying dead, with one barrel of his gun discharged and the contents buried in his body. And the ghost of that man may sometimes be seen, leaning over the low wall, pointing a gun at some object which moves quickly in the long grasses . . .

Warleggan

Even the brilliant sunshine on the day I first visited the Old Rectory here could not dispel the gloom and apprehension and air of apathy that hung over the place like a heavy cloud of doom. Even the rare optimism and charming company of James and Cathy Turner could not relieve the sense of unhappiness that seemed to hang about this place.

◄'Each New Year's Eve, at midnight, a phantom
coach, driven by a headless coachman gallops
through the courtyard of the Molesworth Arms at Wadebridge.'

The last incumbent, the eccentric Rev. Frederick William Densham, who served the parish from 1931 to 1953, is thought to still haunt the house and grounds. The house has a very weird atmosphere; he painted the interior rooms red, yellow and blue—and he painted the interior of the church in the same glaring colours. He built a barbed-wire fence all round the rectory garden, which he guarded with fierce dogs; he refused to hold services at times convenient to his parishioners and generally he lived at odds with the local people. After a church enquiry into his conduct in 1933 the Church Council resigned in a body and never went near the church again. Soon no one went to his services and many entries in the Service Book read on the lines: 'No fog, no wind, no rain, no congregation'. In what surely must have been genuine unhappiness and sorrow he cut out figures in wood and cardboard and fixed them in the pews and to them he preached and offered Absolution.

He named the rooms in the rectory with Biblical names; he painted large pink crosses on the doors; he preserved an ancient hiding place in the old cellars; and eventually he fell down the stairs and died because he could not reach the bell-pull that would summon his servant who was quartered in the stables.

Long before Frederick Densham was here a previous building that occupied the site was lived in by Ralph de Tremur who is thought to have celebrated Black Mass in the church; certainly he burnt the Host . . . small wonder that Warleggan is haunted.

When I was there some years ago the house was empty and the garden overgrown. Both are certainly haunted, I was assured, and there are numerous accounts of the sad, dark figure of Frederick Densham walking where he used to walk, towards the empty church, on moonlit nights, or up the drive to the locked and barred door of the empty rectory; sitting where he used to sit and preaching where he used to preach in his torn cassock and dusty hat.

I heard stories of many odd happenings, some possibly paranormal in origin; and of the strange individuals who are drawn to Warleggan but they never seem to stay very long in this place of ghosts and hollow memories.

The Rev. Densham painted the rooms of Warleggan Rectory red, yellow and blue, and built a barbed wire fence round the garden. ▶

Bodilly Farm, Wendron, where there may be
ghosts and treasure.

Wendron

A few years ago my wife and I sought out Bodilly Farm, reputedly
the scene of a curious manifestation which, perhaps even more
curiously has never been followed up and thoroughly investigated.
We saw the place where treasure may still be hidden but the
occupants at that time were not prepared to co-operate in any
practical investigation of the intriguing story. The case came to my
knowledge through my good friend and Ghost Club member, Air
Commodore R. Carter Jonas who had come across the story as a boy
and had been puzzled and baffled by the tale ever since.

The story goes, according to a one-time Methodist minister of
Goldsithney, that some eighty years ago a miner sought to rent a
house here that was reputed to be haunted and indeed the owner
was reluctant to let the place because so many people had taken it

but never stayed long . . . however the miner ridiculed the idea of ghosts and he and his mother and sister were soon established in the house. At that time it was a quaint place with only two rooms downstairs, but tremendous rooms they were, like great barns. At one end of the room used as a kitchen there was a wide, old-fashioned open fireplace, large enough to seat several people.

A few days after moving in the miner was at work when his mother, sitting at the 'fringle' fire, heard the latch of the door lifted. She looked round and saw, to her surprise, the door open and a black calf walk in, look round and walk out again, carefully latching the door behind it! Thinking she must have been dreaming, she made no mention of the matter when her son returned home later in the day; but from that time onwards weird noises repeatedly disturbed the family at night when they were in bed. The miner did his utmost to fathom the mysterious sounds, searching every corner and crevice of the house but he failed to find any clue or explanation.

Then one night the miner's mother was awakened by the sound of someone in her room and striking a light she was astonished to see three diminutive figures standing in a row beside her bed. She hastily blew out the light and hid among the bedclothes until she heard the figures depart.

A few nights later the performance was repeated and when it happened a third time the old lady plucked up courage to enquire what her visitors wanted. Whereupon one of the unbidden guests replied: 'You are the first who has ever spoken to us and we have come to do you good'.

He then told her to break down the plaster between two windows in her son's bedroom and she would find a place like a chimney and at the bottom of the chimney she must dig until she reached a large stone. Beneath that stone she would find 'abundant wealth for herself and her family'.

So certain was the old lady that this had been no dream and so impressed was she by the earnestness and sincerity of her visitors that she lost no time in relating everything that had happened to her son and daughter, who in turn consulted a second son who lived a few miles away. He too was impressed by the story and they all decided to test its accuracy by breaking into the plaster at the spot that had been indicated.

That night they tore down the plaster between the two windows, which stood in the north wall, and there, sure enough, was a large aperture, exactly as though a chimney had been pierced, although no fireplace existed and the clean state of the stonework suggested that there had never been a fireplace there. By means of a strong rope the miner was lowered into the aperture which he discovered led, like a secret passage, to the ground, where it ended.

Having proved the story to be true so far the excited family soon set to work and shifted an enormous amount of earth and rubble until eventually a huge flat stone or boulder was exposed and it was concluded that this must be the stone that had been referred to. The miner tried working round the stone but soon realized blasting would be necessary to remove the boulder and settle the mystery once and for all. A hole was bored ready for the charge and then it was decided to wait until the following night.

Sadly the next day the miner met with a terrible accident in the mine where he was employed; both his hands were blown off at the wrists and he was almost scalped. When he was carried home his mother prepared a bed for him in the kitchen.

Next day the bedroom was cleared as much as possible, a sheet was tucked up to cover the mouth of the shaft, and the mutilated miner was carried upstairs to his own bedroom. Several of his fellow miners offered to take turns to sit up with their comrade at night and some, more curious than the others, lifted the sheet, discovered the hole and the rumour began to circulate in the immediate area that the injured miner had found a rich lode and was mining on his own account.

After several days, hovering between this world and the next, the miner died and after the funeral, fearing the consequences now that their labours had been discovered, the miner's brother threw as much rubble as he could lay his hands on back into the hole and replastered the wall. So, for the time being, the adventure ended and soon afterwards the old lady and her daughter moved to live with their relative some miles away.

Years later the old lady's grandson, who had heard the story as a boy, enlisted the help of a miner friend and set out to seek for the quaint house and searched for the treasure. They found that the old house had been pulled down and a new and substantial farmhouse built in its place. Their enquiries resulted in the owner allowing them to excavate on the land to see whether they could locate the old shaft. Meanwhile they sought out a former owner who remembered the rumour that the place had been mined and said:

'Perhaps you know that the large slab of slate on which the fire is usually built in the "fringle" opens upon a flight of steps? After the old lady and her daughter left the house a couple moved in and accidentally discovered the flight of steps, obtained a lantern and hurriedly went down to explore; they said they found a large room filled with armour, swords and bronze articles. As they were exploring the place their lantern was suddenly blown out and thinking that they were in a room occupied by ghosts, they hastily rushed up the steps, slammed down the slab of slate to cover the entrance and never told anyone what they had done until the old house had been pulled down and another built in its place'.

The listening miners realized that in all probability the lamp had been extinguished by foul air and they were more convinced than ever that the treasure was there for the finding.

After a lot of hard work they located the foundations of the old house and working round them, were delighted when they hit upon the old shaft, but it ran beneath the existing house and they eagerly sought permission to burrow further in search of the old cellars but the owner became frightened lest the building should be undermined and collapse and nothing would induce him to consent to them delving and excavating underneath his house.

There are stories of the old house being a smugglers' hide-out and the practice of burying treasure was by no means uncommon in smuggling days. So there *may* still be a fortune waiting for someone who is adventurous enough to seek for treasure that seems to have been revealed by a ghost.

When he re-visited Bodilly Farm in 1959 Air Commodore R.C. Jonas was told that the shaft had been filled in and when I was there some years later I was shown a concrete cattle-yard which had, I was told, been built over the shaft. Perhaps some competent metal detector or diviner could locate the exact whereabouts of whatever still lies buried at Bodilly Farm. It seems such a pity not to verify or disprove such a long-standing mystery.

Zennor

Here the best-known of all mermaid stories is commemorated with a carving on a pew in the church. There are several versions of the story but generally it concerns the local vicar, taking a stroll along the beach one day, and being struck by the sound of a gentle voice and discovering a beautiful mermaid. So taken was he by her voice that he persuaded her to attend his church, suitably dressed, and one day a handsome local boy, Matthew Trehella, saw her, fell in love with her, and followed her to the beach, and into the sea—and he has never been seen again; although for many years afterwards and some say to this very day, the sound of sweet singing, a male voice and a female voice, can be heard in Pendour Cove.

Some years after Matthew Trehella disappeared a fishing skipper dropped anchor in Pendour Cove and was surprised to hear a sweet and seductive voice hailing him. When he looked over the side of his boat he was astonished to see a mermaid who popped her head out of the water and complained that he had dropped his anchor across the entrance to her cave beneath the waves and until it was moved she could not reach her lover, Matthew. The skipper obligingly weighed anchor at once!

The mermaid has not been seen again but the unexplained sound of sweet singing is sometimes heard wafting up the rugged headland from the sea.

SELECT BIBLIOGRAPHY

Alexander, Marc, *Ghostly Cornwall,* Pacific Press, 1977,
Haunted Churches and Abbeys of Britain, Arthur Barker,
1978, *Haunted Inns,* Frederick Muller, 1973, *Phantom Britain,*
Frederick Muller, 1975.
Braddock, Joseph, *Haunted Houses,* Batsford, 1956.
Brown, Raymond Lamont, *Phantoms, Legends, Customs and
Superstitions of the Sea,* Patrick Stephens, 1972.
Coxe, Antony D. Hippisley, *Haunted Britain,* Hutchinson, 1973.
du Maurier, Daphne, *Vanishing Cornwall,* Victor Gollancz, 1967.
Deane, Tony, and Shaw, Tony *The Folklore of Cornwall,*
Batsford, 1975
Francis, Di, *Cornish Ghosts,* James Pike, 1977.
Green, Andrew, *Ghosts of Today,* Kaye and Ward, 1980,
Our Haunted Kingdom, Wolfe, 1973.
Hallam, Jack, *The Ghosts' Who's Who,* David and Charles, 1977,
The Haunted Inns of England, Wolfe, 1972.
Hunt, Robert, *Popular Romances of the West of England,* Chatto
and Windus, 1871.
MacGregor, Alasdair Alpin, *The Ghost Book,* Robert Hale, 1955.
Moss, Peter, *Ghosts over Britain,* Elm Tree Books, 1977.
Norman, Diana, *The Stately Ghosts of England,* Frederick Muller,
1963.
Norway, Arthur H., *Highways and Byways in Devon and
Cornwall,* Macmillan, 1922.
Turner, James, *Ghosts in the South West,* David and Charles,
1973.
Underwood, Peter, *A Host of Hauntings,* Leslie Frewin, 1973.
Gazetteer of British Ghosts, Souvenir Press, 1971.
Williams, Michael, *Cornish Mysteries,* Bossiney Books, 1980,
Supernatural in Cornwall, Bossiney Books, 1975.

ACKNOWLEDGEMENTS

The author wishes to thank everyone who has helped him in the compilation of this volume in particular the staff of Cornwall County Libraries, the staff of various National Trust properties and especially Marc Alexander, Mrs Denise Buckridge, Paul Cowling, Antony Hippisley Coxe, the Rev. Peter L. Eustice, Mrs A. Evans, David Eyles, Mrs Julie Frost, Michael Garside, Mrs Govett, A.H. Hammett, Miss Cynthia Hoskin, Air Commodore R.C. Jonas, Mrs Phyllis Julyan, Mrs M.A. King, Lord St Levan, Mr and Mrs T.A. Ley, David Moore, Mrs Marion Grace Paul, Bill Pilgrim, Mrs Margaret Powell, Miss Joan Rendell, Mrs Cathy Turner, A.B. Venning, his publisher Michael Williams and, as always, his wife Joyce Elizabeth.

ALSO AVAILABLE

GHOSTS OF DEVON
by Peter Underwood. 44 photographs and drawings.
Peter Underwood, President of the Ghost Club, writes of the ghostly stories that
saturate the County of Devon, a land full of mystery and of ghostly lore and legend.
'*Packed with photographs, this is a fascinating book.*'
Herald Express

CURIOSITIES OF CORNWALL
by Michael Williams. 62 photographs.
Eccentric architecture; customs—curious, Cornish and Royal; curious characters
and a curiosity that grew into invention and innovation; the deep hole at Delabole;
the question witch or saint? . . . all these and much more prove that Cornwall has
more than her share of curiosities.
'*. . . a fascinating new book . . . avid collectors of off-beat gems of knowledge, whether
they belong to the county or not, will welcome it as a treasure . . .*'
Pamela Leeds, The Western Evening Herald.

STRANGE HAPPENINGS IN CORNWALL
by Michael Williams. 35 photographs.
Strange shapes and strange characters; healing and life after death; reincarnation
and Spiritualism; murders and mysteries are only some of the contents in this
fascinating book.
'*. . . this eerie Cornish collection.*'
David Foot, Western Daily Press

CORNISH MYSTERIES
by Michael Williams. 40 photographs.
Cornish Mysteries is a kind of jig-saw puzzle in words and pictures. The power of
charming, mysterious shapes in the Cornish landscape, the baffling murder case of
Mrs Hearn are just some fascinating ingredients.
'*. . . superstitions, dreams, murder, Lyonesse, the legendary visit of the boy Jesus to
Cornwall, and much else. Splendid, and sometimes eerie, chapters.*'
The Methodist Recorder

LEGENDS OF CORNWALL
by Sally Jones. 60 photographs and drawings.
Brilliantly illustrated with photographs and vivid drawings of legendary characters.
A journey through the legendary sites of Cornwall, beginning at the Tamar and
ending at Land's End.
'*Highly readable and beautifully romantic . . .*'
Desmond Lyons, Cornwall Courier

OTHER BOSSINEY TITLES INCLUDE

A CORNISH CAMERA
by George Ellis and Sarah Foot

VIEWS OF OLD CORNWALL
by Sarah Foot

A CORNISH YEAR BOOK

MY CORNWALL

KING ARTHUR COUNTRY
by Brenda Duxbury, Michael Williams, Colin Wilson

THE CORNISH EDWARDIANS
by David Mudd

THE CRUEL CORNISH SEA
by David Mudd

CASTLES OF CORNWALL
by Mary and Hal Price

CORNISH CHURCHES
by Joan Rendell

POLDARK COUNTRY
by David Clarke

OCCULT IN THE WEST
by Michael Williams

SUPERSTITION AND FOLKLORE
by Michael Williams

SUPERNATURAL IN CORNWALL
by Michael Williams

CORNWALL IN UPROAR
by David Mudd